SIRACUSA GUIDELINES FOR INTERNATIONAL, REGIONAL AND NATIONAL FACT-FINDING BODIES

SIRACUSA GUIDELINES FOR INTERNATIONAL, REGIONAL AND NATIONAL FACT-FINDING BODIES

International Institute of Higher Studies in Criminal Sciences

Edited by M. Cherif BASSIOUNI
and Christina ABRAHAM

intersentia
Cambridge – Antwerp – Portland

Intersentia Publishing Ltd.
Trinity House | Cambridge Business Park | Cowley Road
Cambridge | CB4 0WZ | United Kingdom
tel.: +44 1223 393 753 | email: mail@intersentia.co.uk

Distribution for the UK:
NBN International
Airport Business Centre, 10 Thornbury Road
Plymouth, PL6 7PP
United Kingdom
Tel: +44 1752 202 301 | Fax: +44 1752 202 331
Email: orders@nbninternational.com

Distribution for the USA and Canada:
International Specialized Book Services
920 NE 58th Ave Suite 300
Portland, OR 97213
USA
Tel.: +1 800 944 6190 (toll free)
Email: info@isbs.com

Distribution for Austria:
Neuer Wissenschaftlicher Verlag
Argentinierstraße 42/6
1040 Wien
Austria
Tel.: +43 1 535 61 03 24
Email: office@nwv.at

Distribution for other countries:
Intersentia Publishing nv
Groenstraat 31
2640 Mortsel
Belgium
Tel.: +32 3 680 15 50
Email: mail@intersentia.be

Siracusa Guidelines for International, Regional and National Fact-finding Bodies
Edited by M. Cherif Bassiouni and Christina Abraham

© 2013 International Institute of Higher Studies in Criminal Sciences (ISISC)

www.intersentia.com | www.intersentia.co.uk

Cover photograph: © Chones

ISBN 978-1-78068-193-1
D/2013/7849/109
NUR 828

British Library Cataloguing in Publication Data. A catalogue record for this book is available from the British Library.

No part of this book may be reproduced in any form, by print, photoprint, microfilm or any other means, without written permission from the publisher.

Table of Contents

About the Editors ix
Abbreviations xi
Preface xiii
Drafting Committee of the Siracusa Guidelines xix
Participants of the Meeting of Experts at the
International Institute of Higher Studies in Criminal
Sciences – Siracusa, Italy xxi

Part I: Identification of Issues in Relation to UN Fact-finding Mechanisms 1
   Introduction 3
   International Commissions of Inquiry 8
      Methods and Costs of COIs 11
   Special Procedures 18
      Methods and Costs of Special Procedures 19
   Treaty Bodies 21
      Methods and Costs of the Treaty Body System 22
   De-facto Fact-Finding Missions Undertaken by the UN
   Department of Peacekeeping Operations (DPKO) 27
   National Fact-Finding Bodies 29
   Conclusion 34

Part II: The Siracusa Guidelines 35

Part III: An Empirical Analysis of United Nations Commissions of Inquiry: Toward the Development of a Standardized Methodology 53
   Abstract 55
   Introduction 56
   UN Monitoring, Reporting and Fact-finding Activities 58
   Methods 63
   Results 65
      Mandates 65

State Consent 67
Prior and Simultaneous Investigations 67
Terms of Reference 68
Facts Alleged and Conclusions Reached 69
Investigative Methodology.................................... 69
Commissioners and Mission Personnel 73
Witnesses, Victims and Detainees............................. 75
The Role of Non-Governmental Organizations 78
Recommendations and Follow-up................................ 79
Budgets and Resource Allocation.............................. 80
DISCUSSION ON THE CHALLENGES IN IMPLEMENTING AND
FACILITATING FACT-FINDING MISSIONS........................... 80
Mandates and Terms of Reference 81
Lack of Standardized Methodology Guiding Fact-Finding
Missions... 82
Commissioners and Personnel.................................. 85
Witnesses, Victims and Detainees............................. 87
The Role of NGOs and Members of Civil Society................ 90
Budgets and Resource Allocation.............................. 92
IMPLICATIONS FOR BEST PRACTICE IN FACT-FINDING MISSIONS 93
Mandates... 93
Appointment of Commissioners and Hiring of Mission
Personnel.. 93
Terms of Reference 94
Investigative Methodology and Report Compilation 95
Recommendations Regarding Witnesses and Victims 96
Recommendations Regarding Budgets and Resource Allocation... 97
LIMITATIONS OF THE STUDY 98

**APPENDICES TO THE EMPIRICAL ANALYSIS OF UNITED NATIONS
COMMISSIONS OF INQUIRY** 101
APPENDIX 1: REPORTS EVALUATED IN SAMPLE 103
APPENDIX 2: QUANTITATIVE VARIABLES........................... 107
APPENDIX 3: OPERATIONALIZATION OF QUANTITATIVE VARIABLES. 109
APPENDIX 4: THEMATIC GUIDING QUESTIONS FOR QUALITATIVE
REVIEW... 111

UN DOCUMENTS. 117
UN GENERAL ASSEMBLY RESOLUTION 67/1. 119
REPORT OF THE UN SECRETARY-GENERAL ON DELIVERING
JUSTICE: PROGRAMME OF ACTION TO STRENGTHEN THE RULE OF
LAW AT THE NATIONAL AND INTERNATIONAL LEVEL 125
STATEMENT OF THE UN SECRETARY-GENERAL AT THE HIGH-
LEVEL MEETING OF THE GENERAL ASSEMBLY ON THE RULE OF
LAW, 24 SEPTEMBER 2012. 145
STATEMENT OF ISISC PRESIDENT, PROFESSOR M. CHERIF
BASSIOUNI, AT THE HIGH-LEVEL MEETING OF THE GENERAL
ASSEMBLY ON THE RULE OF LAW, 24 SEPTEMBER 2012 149

ABOUT THE EDITORS

M. CHERIF BASSIOUNI

M. Cherif Bassiouni is *Emeritus* Professor of Law at DePaul University where he taught from 1964-2012. He was a founding member of the International Human Rights Law Institute at DePaul University which was established in 1990. He served as President from 1990-1997 and then President *Emeritus*. In 1972, he was one of the founders of the International Institute of Higher Studies in Criminal Sciences (ISISC) located in Siracusa, Italy, where he served as Dean from 1972-1989 and then as President to date. He also served as the Secretary General of the International Association of Penal Law from 1974-1989 and as President for three five-year terms from 1989-2004 when he was elected Honorary President.

Since 1975, Professor Bassiouni has been appointed to the following United Nations positions: Chair and then member of the Commission of Inquiry for Libya (2011-2012); Independent Expert on Human Rights for Afghanistan (2004-2006); Independent Expert on the Rights to Restitution, Compensation, and Rehabilitation for Victims of Grave Violations of Human Rights and Fundamental Freedoms (1998-2000); Chair, Drafting Committee of the Diplomatic Conference on the Establishment of an International Criminal Court (1998); Vice-Chair of the General Assembly's Preparatory Committee on the Establishment of an International Criminal Court (1996-1998); Vice-Chair of the General Assembly's Ad Hoc Committee on the Establishment of an International Criminal Court (1995); Chair of the Commission of Experts Established Pursuant to Security Council 780 (1992) to Investigate Violations of International Humanitarian Law in the Former Yugoslavia (1993-1994) and the Commission's Special Rapporteur on Gathering and Analysis of the Facts (1992-1993).

He also served as Chair of the Bahrain Independent Commission of Inquiry which was established in 2011.

To date, Professor Bassiouni has authored 27 books, edited 45 books, and authored 265 articles on International Criminal Law, Comparative Criminal Law, Human Rights, and U.S. Criminal Law that have been published in various law journals and books. Additionally, he has written 14 Monographs on such subjects as history, politics, and religion.

CHRISTINA ABRAHAM

Christina Abraham is the international research fellow at the International Institute of Higher Studies in Criminal Sciences (ISISC) in Siracusa, Italy. At ISISC, Ms. Abraham assists in developing programs on the rule of law, international criminal law and human rights, in line with ISISC's mandate. She also conducts research and analytical work on ISISC research programs. Prior to joining ISISC, Ms. Abraham was the Civil Rights Director at the Council on American-Islamic Relations in Chicago (CAIR-Chicago). In 2011, she served as the Chief of Staff for the Bahrain Independent Commission of Inquiry (BICI), an independent commission that investigated human rights abuses in Bahrain after demonstrations calling for government reforms began in February 2011. She is an attorney-at-law and holds a JD from DePaul University and an MA from the University of Chicago.

Abbreviations

COI – Commission of Inquiry
HRC – Human Rights Council
HRTD – Human Rights Treaties Division
ICC – International Criminal Court
ICTR – International Criminal Tribunal for Rwanda
ICTY – International Criminal Tribunal for the former Yugoslavia
MRF – Monitoring, Reporting and Fact-finding
NGO – Non-governmental Organization
OHCHR – Office of the High Commissioner for Human Rights
UDHR – Universal Declaration of Human Rights
UNDPKO – United Nations Department of Peacekeeping Operations
UN – United Nations
UNSG – United Nations Secretary-General
UNGA – United Nations General Assembly
UNSC – United Nations Security Council

Preface

Fact-finding bodies have been and continue to be established in different contexts by a variety of mechanisms. They may be established by the UN, treaty monitoring bodies, regional organizations, governments or national institutions, or NGOs, whether working alone or in collaboration with another body. As a result, the mandates that establish fact-finding bodies include political considerations, but more importantly they lack the specificity related to the professional nature of these bodies' missions. The objectives established for these fact-finding bodies, and more importantly how they function, the expertise of their personnel, the professionalism of their methods, and the resources they have at their disposal, vary significantly. Because each fact-finding situation is sui generis, the mixture of objectives and benefits of fact-finding bodies will differ from situation to situation or from country to country, but most importantly the difference will also be in the manner in which these bodies function. Very often the sui generis nature of fact-finding bodies also leads to ad hoc approaches to their operations. Fact-finding bodies may be purely investigatory, quasi-judicial, or have a truth and reconciliation component attached. Whatever the mechanisms of accountability, the first necessary step is always fact-finding, and these guidelines are concerned primarily with the issue of how to conduct a professional investigatory operation irrespective of what the ultimate purpose is of the data collected, or how the analysis made will be used. This is indispensable to ensure the professionalism of fact-finding operations, the reliability of the data obtained, its credibility, all of which are essential for any subsequent determination of whatever action may be contemplated. It is also the only way in which a comparison can be made of different situations that are the subject of fact-finding inquiries.

Many fact-finding bodies are created to investigate allegations of human rights violations. These fact-finding bodies allow international and national institutions to obtain information on a given situation and may provide advice on actions or remedies that should be taken to avert further conflict, restore stability, promote accountability or support adherence to the rule of law. They have also been useful in establishing a basis for future criminal investigations and prosecutions, whether internationally or nationally, sometimes working alongside domestic and international criminal justice mechanisms. This is in line with the UN General Assembly's Declaration of Basic Principles of Justice for Victims of Crime and Abuse of Power. Human rights fact-finding bodies also provide an important mechanism for bringing closure to the victims of human rights abuse, which is a necessary component of achieving reconciliation, and promoting the right to truth. Finally, fact-finding bodies may also have a monitoring role: to establish whether any breaches of law (whether international humanitarian law, international human rights law, international criminal law or domestic law) have occurred, and investigating and publicizing the facts surrounding those breaches. Fact-finding bodies can also minimize ongoing violations of human rights and enhance compliance with national and international law.

Human rights fact-finding has increasingly become recognized as an important exercise to strengthen and support the rule of law in certain contexts. For example, UN General Assembly Resolution 67/1 emphasized the importance of fact-finding, "including those that investigate patterns of past violations of international human rights law and international humanitarian law and their causes and consequences" as "important tools that can complement judicial processes." Further, the UN Secretary-General has recognized fact-finding as an effective tool to "draw out facts necessary for wider accountability and transitional justice efforts."

Because the political objectives of fact-finding bodies vary from mission to mission, each fact-finding body produces different results. It is therefore difficult to compare the work products of these different missions because each one relies on different financial and human resources, adopts different methodologies, and therefore produces different results. The implication of this is that the work products of these fact-finding bodies cannot necessarily be relied upon by international or national judicial mechanisms such as the International Criminal Court or international and mixed-model tribunals. Also, very often human rights fact-finding bodies do not take into account parallel work conducted by historical or prosecutorial commissions, UN Special Procedures or the fact-finding work conducted within the Treaty Body System. The lack of coordination among these different bodies and inconsistencies in approaches and methodologies may lead to duplicated work and unreliable results. Perhaps an effective way of dealing with this would be to create a permanent body or pool of experts from which individuals could be selected to serve as Commissioners on these human rights fact-finding bodies. Such a system may help guarantee that fact-finding bodies are led by qualified experts, while at the same time ensure a degree of flexibility for mandating bodies to select the experts that best fit each unique situation.

Understandably, there are differences in the goals and missions of different fact-finding bodies, which are reflected in their mandates. Ongoing fact-finding in connection with UN Special Procedures and other mechanisms that fall within the meaning of Special Procedures have developed since the establishment of the United Nations, first under the Commission on Human Rights and the sub-commission on the Prevention of Discrimination and Protection of Minorities, and as of 2005 under the Council on Human Rights. But these are not the only UN bodies that have dealt with fact-finding processes, some like the Security Council Commission established pursuant to Resolution 780 (1992) was probably the most extensive fact-finding operation the United Nations undertook since its establishment. The Commission's two-year work resulted in the longest report published as a Security Council document (3,500 pages with 72,000 documents attached, 300 hours of video tape material, and 3,000 pictures). The work of the Commission resulted in the establishment of the ICTY as noted in the preamble of UN Security Council Resolution 827. As noted in the study made of these different bodies, *An Empirical Analysis of United Nations Commissions of Inquiry: Toward the Development of a Standardized Methodology*, available in this publication, there have been 30 fact-finding bodies established by various United Nations bodies, distinguishable from the continued work of the Special Procedures and Treaty Body System. The way in which these and other bodies conducting human rights fact-finding differ from one another is explored in the study Identification of Issues in Relation to UN Fact-finding Mechanisms, also available in this publication. What both of these studies evidence is the differences that exist both among UN Commissions of Inquiry, and between UN Commissions of Inquiry and other UN fact-finding bodies and procedures. This diversity cannot be explained in professional terms, only in political ones. What these two studies reveal is that there is definitely a need for enhanced professionalization of these fact-finding bodies, notwithstanding the diversity of their origin and the differences in their mandates. Having had the privilege of Chairing and being a member of four official fact-finding bodies, three established by the United Nations for the Former Yugoslavia, Afghanistan, and Libya (of which I was first Chair and then Member), and Chair of the Bahrain Independent Commission of Inquiry (BICI), a national commission, and also head of a private project in Iraq which compiled the oral history of over 5,000 victims of the Saddam regime, I can attest to the problems and difficulties encountered in each one of these fact-finding bodies for the reasons discussed in the two studies contained in this publication.

In developing the Siracusa Guidelines, various best practice documents and training manuals were also reviewed, such as the *Chicago Principles on Post-Conflict Justice*, the *Lund-London Guidelines*, the *Brahimi Report*, the *Belgrade Minimum Rules of Procedure for International Human Rights Fact-Finding Visits*, the *University of Nottingham's Guiding Principles for Human Rights Field Officers Working in Conflict and Post-conflict Environments*, the *OHCHR Training Manual on Human Rights Monitoring*, the *Manual of Operations of the Special Procedures of the HRC*, and the *Institute for International Criminal Investigations' Investigators Manual*, among a number of other materials. The results of the research studies identified above and the review of other best practice documents were used to prepare the first draft of the Guidelines.

ISISC then organized a Meeting of Experts to review the draft Guidelines. This Meeting brought together over 70 international judges and prosecutors, UN officials, academics and other experts to review the Guidelines and provide comments. After the conclusion of the Meeting, a Drafting Committee composed of highly experienced academics, jurists and legal practitioners met to review the comments made by experts and deliberate upon the draft Guidelines. A subsequent draft of the Siracusa Guidelines was circulated to participants of the Meeting of Experts. Their comments were received by the Drafting Committee, who then adopted a final draft of the Guidelines. The experts and Drafting Committee members have contributed to this endeavor in their personal capacities. Although nothing in this undertaking is attributable to any government, UN agency, or institution with which any of the participants are affiliated, their input has been of immense value in developing the Guidelines.

The Siracusa Guidelines seek to promote an effective approach to human rights fact-finding based upon compliance with international best practices. The Guidelines have been developed as a practical guide for establishing and operating a fact-finding body investigating human rights violations. The Guidelines are intended to aid a mandating body in establishing a mandate and selecting Commissioners, as well as to aid Commissioners and staff in effectively carrying out their mandate. They are therefore designed to address the three main phases of the life of a fact-finding body: 1) establishment; 2) investigation; and 3) reporting and follow-up.

The structure of the Guidelines recognizes that each mission operates within different contexts. The effectiveness of any fact-finding body requires that it consider this context in its establishment and operation. As such, the Guidelines contain a degree of flexibility, and all guidelines may not apply in all situations equally. Because of the variety of different contextual possibilities, the applicability of each Guideline may not be reflected in the text; however, compliance with the Guidelines will result in enhanced credibility and effectiveness for missions. The Siracusa Guidelines have been developed keeping in mind the experiences of UN and other fact-finding bodies, including the BICI, which reviewed other fact-finding body experiences before establishing its mandate and internal rules and procedures. The Guidelines are therefore intended, amongst other things, to ensure that the positive elements and lessons learned from these fact-finding bodies are preserved and readily accessible for future missions.

ISISC and I extend our deepest appreciation to the participants of the Meeting of Experts and to the Drafting Committee, whose names follow.

M. Cherif Bassiouni
President, ISISC; Emeritus Professor of Law and President Emeritus, International Human Rights Law Institute, DePaul University College of Law; Honorary President, International Association of Penal Law

DRAFTING COMMITTEE OF THE SIRACUSA GUIDELINES

PROFESSOR M. CHERIF BASSIOUNI, CHAIR
President, International Institute of Higher Studies in Criminal Sciences; Emeritus Professor of Law, DePaul University College of Law; former Chair, Bahrain Independent Commission of Inquiry; former Chair and then Member, UN Commission of Inquiry for Libya; former UN Independent Expert on the Situation of Human Rights in Afghanistan; former Chairman, UN Security Council Commission to Investigate Violations of International Humanitarian Law in the Former Yugoslavia; former Independent Expert for the Commission on Human Rights on The Rights to Restitution, Compensation and Rehabilitation for Victims of Grave Violations of Human Rights and Fundamental Freedoms (United States/Egypt)

H.E. COMMISSIONER KAREN ABUZAYD
Commissioner, UN Commission of Inquiry for Syria; former Commissioner-General, UNRWA (United States)

DR. MAHNOUSH H. ARSANJANI
Judge, World Bank Administrative tribunal; Former Vice President, The American Society of International Law; former Director of Codification, Office of Legal Affairs for the United Nations; former Commissioner, Bahrain Independent Commission of Inquiry (Iran)

DR. TARIQ BALOCH
Advisor, Freshfields Brukhaus and Derringer (United Kingdom)

H.E. Serge Brammertz
Prosecutor, ICTY; former Federal Prosecutor, Kingdom of Belgium (Belgium)

H.E. Philippe Kirsch
Former Commissioner, Bahrain Independent Commission of Inquiry; Former Member and Chair, UN Commission of Inquiry on Libya; Former President, International Criminal Court; Former Ambassador of Canada to Sweden (Canada/Belgium)

Ms. Christina Abraham, Secretary
Siracusa Guidelines Project Coordinator; International Research Fellow, International Institute of Higher Studies in Criminal Sciences; Attorney-at-Law, Chicago, USA

Participants of the Meeting of Experts at the International Institute of Higher Studies in Criminal Sciences – Siracusa, Italy

Participants of the Meeting of Experts on the Establishment of Principles and Best Practices for International and National Commissions of Inquiry, Siracusa, Italy, 14 – 17 March 2013.

1. H.E. Commissioner Karen AbuZayd, Commissioner, UN Commission of Inquiry for Syria; former Commissioner-General, UNRWA (United States).
2. Judge Khaled Ahmed, Judge, Cairo Court of Appeals; Legal Advisor to the Supreme Judicial Council of Bahrain Former Chief Investigator, Bahrain Independent Commission of Inquiry (Egypt).
3. H.E. Judge Walid Akoum, Judge, Trial Chamber, Special Tribunal for Lebanon (Lebanon).
4. Ms. Elham Alshejni, Director of Human Rights, League of Arab States (Yemen).
5. Ms. Elizabeth Andersen, Executive Director and Executive Vice President of the American Society of International Law (United States).
6. Dr. Kjell Anderson, Senior Researcher, The Hague Institute for Global Justice (The Netherlands).
7. Dr. Mahnoush H. Arsanjani, Judge, World Bank Administrative Tribunal; Former Vice President, The American Society of International Law; former Director of Codification, Office of Legal Affairs for the United Nations; former Commissioner, Bahrain Independent Commission of Inquiry (United States/Iran).
8. Dr. Tariq Baloch, Advisor, Freshfields Brukhaus and Derringer (United Kingdom).
9. Ms. Shamila Batohi, Senior Legal Advisor and Head of the Legal Advisory Section, Office of the Prosecutor, International Criminal Court (South Africa).
10. H.E. Serge Brammertz, Prosecutor, ICTY (Belgium).
11. Professor Claude Bruderlein, Senior Researcher, Program on Humanitarian Policy and Conflict Research, Harvard University; Strategic Advisor, International Committee of the Red Cross (United States).
12. H.E. Dr. Ali Bin Fadhel Al Buainain, Attorney General, Bahrain (Bahrain).
13. Ms. Anna Capello, Head of the Division of Confidence-Building Measures, Directorate of Political Advice, Council of Europe (Switzerland).
14. Professor Andrew Clapham, Professor of International Law, Geneva Graduate Institute of International Studies (United Kingdom).
15. Professor José-Luis De La Cuesta Arzamendi, President, Association Internationale de Droit Pénal; Director, Instituto Vasco de Criminologia, Basque University of San Sebastian (Spain).
16. Judge Terje Einarsen, Judge, Galuting High Court, Norway (Norway).

17. Mr. Georg Fliege, Police Reform Adviser, Standing Police Capacity of the Police Division of the Office of Rule of Law and Security Institutions (OROLSI), U.N. Department of Peacekeeping Operations (Germany).
18. Mr. Rob Grace, Project Coordinator and Researcher, Monitoring, Reporting and Fact-Finding Project, Program on Humanitarian Policy and Conflict Research, Harvard University (United States).
19. Professor Larissa van den Herik, Professor of Public International Law, Grotius Centre for International Legal Studies, Leiden University (The Netherlands).
20. H.E. Hassan Bubacar Jallow, Prosecutor, International Criminal Tribunal for Rwanda (Gambia).
21. H.E. Philippe Kirsch, Former Commissioner, Bahrain Independent Commission of Inquiry; Former Member and Chair, UN Commission of Inquiry on Libya; Former President, International Criminal Court; Former Ambassador of Canada to Sweden (Canada/Belgium).
22. Professor Sarah Knuckey, Director, Initiative on Human Rights Fact-Finding (Center for Human Rights and Global Justice, NYU); Adjunct Professor of Clinical Law (New York University School of Law); Advisor, UN Special Rapporteur Inquiry into Drone Strikes and Targeted Killings (United States).
23. Ms. Britta Madsen, Project Coordinator, Rule of Law Training Program, Center for International Peace Operations (Germany).
24. Dean Gregory Mark, Dean, DePaul University College of Law (United States).
25. H.E. Dr. Ali Bin Mohsen Bin Fetais Al Marri, Attorney General, Qatar (Qatar).
26. H.E. Professor Juan Mendez, Visiting Professor of Law, American University, Washington College of Law; UN Special Rapporteur on Torture and Other Cruel, Inhuman and Degrading Treatment or Punishment; Co-Chair of the Human Rights Institute of the International Bar Association; former Special Advisor on Prevention to the Prosecutor of the International Criminal Court (Argentina).
27. H.E. Judge Theodor Meron, President of the International Criminal Tribunal for the former Yugoslavia; Presiding Judge of the Appeals Chambers of the International Criminal Tribunal for Rwanda and the ICTY; President of the Mechanism for International Criminal Tribunals (United States).
28. H.E. Judge Howard Morrison, Judge, Trial Chambers, International Criminal Tribunal for the former Yugoslavia (United Kingdom).

29. Professor Vitit Muntarbhorn, Commissioner, UN Commission of Inquiry on Syria; Former Special Rapporteur on the Situation of Human Rights in the Democratic People's Republic of Korea; UN Committee of Experts on Recommendations of the International Labour Organization; Professor of Law, Chulalongkorn University (Thailand).
30. Mr. Daragh Murray, Programme Director, Human Rights Clinic, Human Rights Centre, University of Essex (United Kingdom).
31. Mr. Constantine Partasides, Partner, Freshfields Brukhas and Derringer (United Kingdom).
32. Dr. Gisela Perren-Klingler, President, International Humanitarian Fact-Finding Commission (Switzerland).
33. H.E. Ambassador Stephen J. Rapp, Ambassador at Large Office of Global Criminal Justice, U.S Department of State, former Chief Prosecutor for the Special Court for Sierra Leone (United States).
34. Mr. Ravi K. Reddy, Legal Affairs Officer, Standing Police Capacity of the Police Division of the Office of Rule of Law and Security Institutions (OROLSI), U.N. Department of Peacekeeping Operations (India).
35. Ms. Mona Rishmawi, Chief of the Rule of Law, Equality and Non-Discrimination Branch, Research and Right to Development Division, Office of the High Commissioner for Human Rights (Egypt).
36. Professor Amr Shalakany, Aga Khan Visiting Distinguished Professor of Islamic Humanities, Brown University; Associate Professor of Law, American University in Cairo (Egypt).
37. Dr. Jan-Michael Simon, Head of the Department for Latin America, Max-Planck Institute for Foreign and International Criminal Law (Germany).
38. Dr. Elin Skaar, Senior Researcher, Coordinator: Rights and Legal Institutions, Chr. Michelsen Institute (Norway).
39. Professor Elies van Sliedregt, Dean of the Faculty of Law and Professor of Criminal Law, Vrije Universiteit Amsterdam (The Netherlands).
40. Professor Carsten Stahn, Professor of International Criminal Law and Global Justice – Grotius Centre for International Legal Studies, Leiden University (The Netherlands).
41. H.E. Judge Cuno Tarfusser, Second Vice-President, ICC (Italy).
42. Judge Jean-François Thony, Procureur Général, Colmar; Vice-President ISISC; Vice-President AIDP (France).
43. Professor John Vervaele, Professor of Economic and European Criminal Law, Willem Pompe Institute, Utrecht University; Vice-President and Director of the Scientific Committee of the AIDP; Member, Board of Directors, ISISC (The Netherlands).

44. Professor Eric Wiebelhaus-Brahm, Director of International Affairs, Florida State University (United States).
45. Professor Ellen Yee, Professor of Law, Drake University (United States).

Delegation from Bahrain

1. Ms. Dana Rashed Al-Zayani, Head of the Follow Up Unit (Bahrain).
2. Mr. Nawaf Hamza, Head of the Special Investigation Unit (Bahrain).

Delegation from Qatar

1. Mr. Fras Ahmed, Head of International Relations, Public Prosecution (Qatar).
2. Mr. Fahad Al Athba, Chief Prosecutor (Qatar).
3. Mr. Khalid Al Kotoub, Expert, Office of the Attorney General (Qatar).
4. Mr. Abdul Hakim Amer Al Sayeri, Undersecretary, Office of Affairs, Office of the Attorney General (Qatar).

Observers

1. Mr. Husam Alkatlabi, Researcher and Data Analyst, Syrian Justice and Accountability Center (United States/Syria).
2. Mr. Francis Arthur, Researcher, MSW (cand), Dominican University (United States).
3. Mr. Ari Bassin, Action Officer, United States Department of State (United States).
4. Ms. Maxine Davis, Researcher, MSW (cand), Dominican University (United States).
5. Ms. Catherine Harwood, Ph.D. (cand) and Researcher, Grotius Center for International Legal Studies, Leiden University (New Zealand).
6. Dr. Ekkehart Muller-Rappard, former Director of Human Rights, Office of the Council of Europe (France).
7. Mr. Ahmed Rehab, Executive Director, Council on American-Islamic Relations – Chicago Chapter (United States/Egypt).
8. Mr. Laith Saud, Ph.D. (cand) University of Chicago; Lecturer, DePaul University (United States/Iraq).
9. Mr. Wael Sawah, Project Director, Syrian Justice and Accountability Center (United States/Syria).
10. Dr. Leticia Villarreal Sosa, PhD, LCSW; Assistant Professor, Dominican University (United States).

11. Dean Charlie Stoops, Dean, Graduate School of Social Work, Dominican University (United States).
12. Mr. Yaser Tabbara, Legal Advisor, Syrian National Coalition (United States/Syria).

ISISC STAFF

1. Ms. Christina Abraham, Project Coordinator, International Research Fellow, ISISC; Attorney-at-Law, Chicago, Illinois (United States).
2. Ms. Assia Buonocore, ISISC Head of Secretariat (Italy).
3. Ms. Jessica DeWalt, Attorney-at-Law, Chicago, Research Assistant to Professor Bassiouni (United States).
4. Ms. Stefania Lentinello, ISISC Program Officer (Italy).
5. Ms. Michelle Martin, PhD (cand), MSW, MSocSci; Lecturer, Dominican University Graduate School of Social Work (United States).
6. Dr. Filippo Musca, Acting Scientific Director, ISISC (Italy/United Kingdom).

Part I:

Identification of Issues in Relation to UN Fact-finding Mechanisms

Identification of Issues in Relation to UN Fact-finding Mechanisms

Prepared by M. Cherif Bassiouni[1] & Christina Abraham[2]

Introduction

There exist a number of different fact-finding mechanisms throughout the UN system, but they typically share two common features. First, their establishment is often driven by political considerations. Second, whether in establishment or operation, these mechanisms are plagued with problems resulting from their *ad hoc* nature. As is often observed about the UN system, the various agencies and bodies that make up the human rights enforcement system operate as separate units, rather than as cogs in one unified machine. The problems that result are increasingly more and more difficult to ignore, as conflicts throughout the world have had devastating effects upon civilian populations and the world's institutions have failed to adequately respond to them in a consistent and systematic manner.[3] Today, the UN recognizes the

---

[1] President, International Institute of Higher Studies in Criminal Sciences; Emeritus Professor of Law, DePaul University College of Law; former Chair, Bahrain Independent Commission of Inquiry; former Chair and then Member, UN Commission of Inquiry for Libya; former UN Independent Expert on the Situation of Human Rights in Afghanistan; former Chairman, UN Security Council Commission to Investigate Violations of International Humanitarian Law in the Former Yugoslavia; former Independent Expert for the Commission on Human Rights on The Rights to Restitution, Compensation and Rehabilitation for Victims of Grave Violations of Human Rights and Fundamental Freedoms.

[2] Siracusa Guidelines Project Coordinator; International Research Fellow, International Institute of Higher Studies in Criminal Sciences; former Chief of Staff, Bahrain Independent Commission of Inquiry; Attorney-at-Law.

[3] The international community was "surprised" – assuming that is an appropriate word for governments that were often willfully ignorant – by the 1994 genocide in Rwanda, where, in some four months an estimated 800,000 people were killed, Darfur, where between 2004 and 2008 roughly 300,000 people were killed and up to two million made refugees (Olivier Degomme, 'Patterns of Mortality Rates in Darfur Conflict', *The Lancet*, 23 January 2010; Reuters, UN refugee chief warns of Darfur "catastrophe", 8 September 2006), or the situation in the southern provinces of the Congo, where tribal conflict is estimated to have taken the lives of many thousands of persons (where we

Intersentia 3

need to improve these mechanisms as a part of its initiative to implement and support Rule of Law programs throughout the world. However, in order to effectively accomplish this, a new vision is necessary, and a comprehensive strategic approach must be conducted at the highest level of the UN system, assessing its various different parts.

Currently, there are a handful of missions and operations with fact-finding components within the UN system that each function completely independently from one another. The bodies establishing them have different overall mandates, goals and methods. Even where the establishing body is the same, internal political considerations often affect how a mission is established, what resources it will be provided and what objectives are set out for it.[4] As a result, these mechanisms, although having the overlapping function of investigating human rights issues, produce various missions and operations whose scope, methods, resources and outcomes are different.[5] Consequently, the diversity in methods and outcomes severely undercuts the efficacy of these missions and wastes human and financial resources on duplicative work.

Within the UN structure, fact-finding can be conducted within the framework of a Commission of Inquiry, Special Procedures mandate, an activity under the Treaty Body System, or within the operations of the Department of Peacekeeping Operations (DPKO). In each of these types of operations, each mandate, and its resulting mission, will depend upon the political considerations that have shaped the decisions of the body

---

lack the specifics to produce even an educated estimate of victims due to lack of interest by the international community). These are only a few of the 313 conflicts which have occurred between 1948 and 2008 and which have resulted in the death of 92 million persons.

[4] This is evident in the resistance of States to the binding legal effect of the Responsibility to Protect. 2005 World Summit Outcome, paras. 138–39, 15 September 2005, A/60/L.1; The International Commission on Intervention and State Sovereignty, *The Responsibility to Protect*, 2001; M. Cherif Bassiouni, "Advancing the Responsibility to Protect through International Criminal Justice" in *Responsibility to Protect: The Global Moral Compact for the 21st Century*, Palgrave McMillan (Richard H. Cooper and Juliette Voinov Kohler, eds. 2009); Gareth Evans and Mohamed Sanhoun, "The Responsibility to Protect", *Foreign Affairs* 81, 2002; Ramesh Thakur, *The United Nations, Peace and Security: From Collective Security to the Responsibility to Protect*, Cambridge University Press (2006); James Pattinson, *Humanitarian Intervention and the Responsibility to Protect: Who Should Intervene?*, Oxford University Press (2010); William Schabas, "Preventing Genocide and Mass Killing: The Challenge for the United Nations", Minority Rights Group International (2005); Rebecca Hamilton, "The Responsibility to Protect, from Document to Doctrine – But What of Implementation?" *Harvard Human Rights Journal* 19 (2006).

[5] M. Cherif Bassiouni, *A Critical Introduction Assessment of the UN Human Rights Mechanisms*, in NEW CHALLENGES FOR THE UN HUMAN RIGHTS MACHINERY (M. Cherif Bassiouni & William Schabas eds., Intersentia 2011).

establishing it. These political considerations influence the type and scope of financial and logistical support the operation will receive, such as the type and scope of service it will receive from the UN Secretariat. Additionally, factors such as the cooperation of the State in which the mission is to be carried out and the availability of adequate specialized personnel also affect the product of the mission. Very often, these factors contribute to the way in which methods of investigation and operation develop. Because each mission is established in an *ad hoc* manner, and its mandate, structure and resources are established "from scratch" each time, each develops its own methods and techniques, some more effectively than others.

There are many specifics that contribute to the divergences that exist in the way that the different missions and operations function, and consequently the outcomes they produce. In this connection, it is important to note that even within the OHCHR, which is required to service most of the mechanisms mentioned above, there is no uniform method of operation. This goes even to the most elementary aspects of systems such as having a uniform database program. Often, even when proposals to address these issues are put forth by high-level UN officials, they face resistance by Member States seeking to preserve the status quo for political reasons. The unfortunate, yet inescapable truth about the UN is that *realpolitik* and excessive bureaucracy always trump efficacy.

As a result of this situation, and the logistical problems that go hand-in-hand with it, mandate holders have increasingly relied on second-hand information from NGOs and the media to conduct their work. The number of Geneva based NGOs has increased from less than 100 in the 1950s to more than 300 today[6] and human rights work in Geneva has become dominated by NGOs, particularly the larger ones with economic and human resources so significant that they can provide alternative sources of fact-finding and information for the UN's human rights institutions and mandate holders. While the contributions of these NGOs alleviate some of the burden of mandate holders, especially in light of the limited resources already allocated to them, and provide Member States and the international community with important resources and data, their methods may not adhere to the same standards of objectivity and independence with which UN-based staff are expected to be bound by.

Moreover, the costs of the different operations vary from mission to mission, and from establishing body to establishing body. For example, the UN allocates over 7 billion USD to the DPKO. Treaty bodies receive

---

[6] Why Geneva? International Organizations & NGOs, available at: www.whygeneva.ch/index.php?option=com_content&task=view&id=839&Itemid=229&lang=en.

39.3 million USD and Special Procedures 13 million USD. Commissions of Inquiry (COIs), which are perhaps the most *ad hoc* of these mechanisms, especially in terms of establishment, range from between 2 to 5 million USD, depending upon the number of missions in operation in a given year. It is especially difficult to articulate an average budget for COIs because their missions are established by different agencies and bodies within the UN system, and their budget information is not always made public. Generally, within these different missions operating under different agencies and bodies, the resources allocated mission by mission vary depending upon the significance it receives from the entity that establishes it.

The research reflected in this paper indicates a number of key findings with respect to these various mechanisms:

COIs established by the UN share no consistency in terms of establishment, operations, methods or end products. They are, in nearly every sense of the term, *ad hoc*. In establishment, there is no consistency in terms of who the mandating body is or the scope and clarity of the mandate that is issued. With respect to their operations, there is no consistent method of investigation. COI reports often do not specify or define a set standard of proof, and among the body of COI literature there is no consistency in the use of standards of proof. Many reports do not articulate investigation methodology, and those that do rarely provide information that is explicit. The result is that final reports vary in terms of the quantity and quality of information provided. Moreover, the recommendations provided by COIs are not consistently followed. Whether recommendations are followed is often largely contingent upon the political motivations of the mandating body, the cooperation of the State under investigation, and whether the findings of the COI have been deemed legitimate by relevant parties.

Special Procedures mandate holders tend to be more isolated within the UN system. They receive their mandates from the HRC, but the incorporation of their findings is not systematized within the UN structure. States have no obligation to apply recommendations put forth by a Special Procedures mandate holder, and the political will to apply recommendations, or even respond to communications, is often minimal. In fact, a majority of communications sent to governments for all thematic mandates are disregarded, and in many country-specific mandates, mandate holders are not even allowed access into the country in question.

Within the *Treaty Body System*, fact-finding takes the shape of country visits now incorporated into six of the treaty bodies (although it has yet to enter into force for two of them). It is unclear the extent to which methods and standards for country visits have been developed. Additionally, problems persist with respect to what constitutes the crux of the treaty body system: namely, the receipt and review of country reports and individual communications. The treaty body system, as it currently stands, can only function because of a striking 84 percent rate of noncompliance in reporting. Moreover, there is no systematized collaboration between treaty bodies and Special Procedures with overlapping mandates, and because recommendations and observations put forth by treaty bodies are not binding upon State Parties, they are often ignored or insufficiently implemented.

DPKO operations conduct fact-finding with respect to assessment missions that are used to make tactical decisions and provide recommendations to the UN Security Council and the UN Secretary-General on how to address a situation. However, little information is known about the methods or even contents and results of these fact-finding operations as they constitute the most secretive and politically attuned type of operation. What is known about these operations is that they too suffer from similar problems with respect to *ad hoc* establishment, redundancies and lack of coordination between other UN agencies and bodies, and lack of systematized financial and logistical support.

This means that a significant amount of work must be done before the UN can meet its objective of incorporating effective fact-finding operations into its Rule of Law initiatives. The UN's recognition of the importance of Rule of Law initiatives is a necessary beginning toward what will hopefully become an important evolution for the organization as it struggles to maintain its relevance in a globalized world.[7] In order to accomplish this, a vision must be conceived and shared by the international community before a comprehensive strategic plan can be established and executed. In the meantime, the various components of the UN system will continue to address issues of Rule of Law, particularly in the areas of peace-keeping operations, human rights and social development. The agencies directly involved are the United Nations Development Programme (UNDP), the United Nations Department of Peacekeeping Operations (DPKO), the United Nations Office on Drugs and Crime (UNODC), and the United Nations Office of the High Commissioner for Human Rights (OHCHR). At present, each of these agencies and bodies function separately from one another, without much coordination, although they frequently overlap as to their missions and functions. Leaving aside the issues of efficiencies and

---

[7] BASSIOUNI, *supra* note 3, at 8.

costs, this overlap has also been a contributing factor to the reduction of their successes.

INTERNATIONAL COMMISSIONS OF INQUIRY

Commissions of Inquiry (COIs) are fact-finding mechanisms intended to correct violations of human rights and humanitarian law by investigating and reporting on a particular situation and providing recommendations to the mandating body.[8] Although specific objectives vary by context, the purpose of a COI may include promoting human rights, fostering national reconciliation, identifying needs for reform and conflict resolution in specific circumstances, attributing responsibility for violations and informing the general public of certain situations. COIs are quasi-judicial in that they must adopt an evidence gathering/review methodology in order to determine the most effective route for ensuring accountability or corrective action based in the law, but they do not have the power to impose criminal fines or sentences.[9] COIs may be mandated by an organ of the UN, a regional organization or a national government.[10]

Fact-finding missions have been increasingly used by the United Nations, regional organizations and national governments for the purpose of gathering reliable information and making recommendations to a mandating body so that it may effectively and lawfully respond to a particular situation. A fact-finding mission, when conducted optimally, can potentially aid in averting protracted conflicts that are damaging to a society in terms of human, institutional and economic costs. However, in order for the findings and recommendations of fact-finding missions to be accepted, they must first be recognized as legitimate by all relevant parties. Typically, the recognition of a fact-finding mission as legitimate hinges upon the methods under which the mission was established and operated.

Because COIs tend to be established after specific incidents in particularized contexts, their creation and operation has tended to be *ad hoc*, and even those established within the UN infrastructure operate independent of one another, develop different methods of investigation, and produce different work products. The international community's struggle

---

[8] Program on Humanitarian Policy and Conflict Research, Harvard University, *Building Effective Monitoring, Reporting and Fact-Finding Mechanisms* 13 (2012) (hereinafter "HPCR Working Paper").
[9] *Id.*
[10] *Id.*

to develop comprehensive and universal guidelines for conducting such missions has ultimately undermined the potential effect of this mechanism.

Within the UN system, COIs are typically mandated either by the Human Rights Council (HRC), the General Assembly (UNGA) or the Security Council (UNSC). Since the formation of the HRC in 2006, it has mandated nine COIs.[11] Beginning from 1992, the UNSC has mandated five COIs.[12]

Because COIs are a product of the current international world order, they have developed in the same *ad hoc* and politically motivated manner as many other international mechanisms. There is no central mandating agency or institution that oversees implementation, although UN-mandated COIs benefit from the logistical support of the Office of the High Commissioner for Human Rights (OHCHR). In 2006, the OHCHR even established a Rapid Response Unit, from which staff members could be deployed for missions, thereby saving time and allowing for faster dispatching. However, the infrastructure from which each COI must operate is still built "from scratch", as there is no central institutionalized structure that exists to date. This contributes to problems in varying methods of investigation, delays in dispatch, and hinders the establishment of a growing body of work from which past lessons can be incorporated and used to better future missions (i.e. the development of institutional memory).

The problems stemming from the *ad hoc* creation of COIs are further exacerbated by the bureaucratic practices and procedures of the UN system via the Secretariat. For example, commissioners of a UN-established COI often have little to no input on the selection of staff, the arrangement of logistical matters, or even administrative decisions affecting the daily operations of the mission. Further, matters that may arise that have not been foreseen by the existing bureaucratic framework of the UN often result in

---

[11] The COIs mandated by the HRC are: 1) the Fact-Finding Mission on the human rights situation in the Occupied Palestinian Territories; 2) High Level Commission of Inquiry on Lebanon; 3) High-Level Fact-Finding Mission to Beit Hanoun; 4) High Level Mission of Human Rights in Darfur; 5) United Nations Fact-Finding Mission on the Gaza Conflict; 6) the Flotilla International Fact-Finding Mission; 7) United Nations International Commission of Inquiry on Libya; 8) Independent International Commission of Inquiry on Côte d'Ivoire; and 9) the Independent International Commission of Inquiry on Syria.

[12] The COIs mandated by the UNSC are: 1) Commission of Experts for the former Yugoslavia; 2) Independent Inquiry into the actions of the United Nations during the 1994 Genocide in Rwanda; 3) International Commission of Inquiry established under Resolution 1012 (1995) Concerning Burundi; 4) International Commission of Inquiry mandated to establish the facts and circumstances of the events of 28 September 2009 in Guinea; and 5) Independent Investigation Commission regarding the assassination of the former President of Lebanon, Rafiq Hariri.

delays or roadblocks to implementing pragmatic solutions to those matters if the proposed solutions are not already contained within the system's procedures.

That COIs are quasi-judicial means that they are also quasi-political. Whether the mandating body is an organ of the UN, a regional body or a national government, motivations for establishing a COI are inherently political. Even decisions regarding how to structure, support and finance COIs can be influenced by political considerations.

By way of example, the UNSC established two fact-finding bodies in 1992 and 1994 in connection with conflicts in the former Yugoslavia and Rwanda, respectively. The first in 1992 was the Commission of Experts pursuant to UN Security Council Resolution 780 (1992) and consisted of five members with an open-ended mandate to investigate all violations of international humanitarian law in the former Yugoslavia during the course of the conflict which existed at the time (which had begun one year prior). The UNSC did not provide an end-date to the work of the Commission, nor did it provide for any limits or guidelines on methods. This was understandable at the time, since the mandate was the first to be adopted by the UN since the end of World War II, after a relatively long period of time in which the pursuit of international criminal justice had been stalled as a result of the Cold War. This mandate therefore broke the ice that existed between 1947 and 1992.

The UNSC did not provide the Commission with any resources, which for all practical purposes meant that its broad mandate could not be accomplished. At no time during the tenure of the Commission did the UNSC provide for funding, although it could have done so from the peacekeeping operations budget. The UNSC also did not authorize the Secretary-General to seek funding from the General Assembly through the normal funding procedure by way of the Fifth Committee. It also did not allow the Commission to establish a voluntary trust fund through which contributions by States could be made. The Commission thus had to use a great deal of ingenuity in order to obtain both private funding sources as well as government contributions to carry out its mission and to conduct its field operations. The Commission's mandate was never formally terminated by the UNSC, but instead by an administrative decision taken by the Office of Legal Affairs (OLA) and therefore presumably authorized by the UN Secretary-General. The Commission had – in its interim report of February 1992 – urged the UNSC to establish an *ad hoc* tribunal for the former Yugoslavia, which led to the UNSC's adoption of Resolution 827 establishing the ICTY. The winding down of the Commission was deemed a transitional matter insofar as it was assumed that the ICTY prosecutor would have continued to carry out the investigative functions of the Commission of Experts. The fact that this did not occur is not particularly relevant to the issue of the legal validity of the manner in which the UNSC-established Commission is terminated by what was in fact an administrative decision. Nevertheless, the work of the Commission was not lost as it provided the factual and evidentiary basis for the ICTY's beginnings.

In contrast, the Commission established by the UNSC to investigate facts in Rwanda was given a limited mandate of three months. It too produced a final report, but its funding was provided by the UN Secretary-General. The work of that Commission also benefited the Prosecutor of the ICTR, but it is clear that by comparing the duration of the two missions, the scope of their work, and the amount of evidence and information obtained, that the first was disproportionately larger in scale than the latter. One could conclude that the facts were more complex in the context of the former Yugoslavia in that the conflict had lasted longer and that the investigation by the Commission of Experts took place during an ongoing conflict; while, in Rwanda the conflict had ended when the Commission began its investigation. The purpose of this description is to show how in fact there is a divergence in every possible respect between these two investigative commissions, notwithstanding the fact that they were established by the same body within the same relative time period, and there is no real rational explanation for these differences.

Methods and Costs of COIs

Once established, in order for COIs to effectively meet their objectives, it is imperative that they are considered legitimate by all parties involved. This means that, despite their political beginnings, a COI must transcend political matters and operate with neutrality, impartiality and independence. Because COIs, regardless of the mandating bodies, are typically established in an *ad hoc* manner, a variety of operating, investigative and analytical methods have been utilized by different bodies. These wide divergences in methodology make COIs susceptible to politically-motivated efforts to undermine their legitimacy, raise concerns over the ability of other missions or mechanisms to rely on their findings, and ultimately hinder the process of implementing recommendations. Furthermore, inconsistent methodologies make it more difficult to transfer the information compiled by the COI to a subsequent enforcement mechanisms such as a court or tribunal, thereby hindering the potential for complementarity and cooperation among COIs and judicial bodies.

A recent study conducted by researchers at Dominican University, evaluating 31 COIs, all-but-one UN-commissioned, revealed the disparity between methods and outputs within the UN system. The results of the study are summarized as follows:[13]

- There is no set timeframe for the operation of COIs. Twelve COIs (37.5 percent) did not even report information on the duration of the investigation. The average length of operation as 137.9 days, but missions ranged from 9 days to 526 days.
- The average length of a final report was 95.2 pages. Final reports ranged from 16 pages to 575 pages.
- Most reports (84.4 percent) included a comprehensive summary of facts and 93.8 percent included a statement about the human rights violations involved. However, only eight reports (25 percent) included information about the submission of evidence.
- All of the reports evaluated indicated whether the State under investigation consented to the COI. The research indicated that most States (71.9 percent) consented to the COI investigation. However, 53.12 percent of reports did not mention whether a Terms of Engagement agreement existed between the UN and the subject State.
- A striking 65.6 percent of reports failed to provide a description of the investigative methodology. Of the 34.4 percent that did include a section on methodology, most were brief and failed to include explicit information on how the investigators obtained, evaluated and analyzed evidence.
- Of the COIs evaluated, 87.5 percent reported having access to witnesses and victims. Only 21.9 percent of reports specified whether witnesses and victims were interviewed in private. Only 21.9 percent of reports indicated whether any provisions were made for witness and victim safety. Only five reports (15.6 percent) included specific information on interview methods.
- Over half, 65.6 percent, of reports indicated whether the COI was granted access to physical sites (i.e. schools, hospitals, prisons, etc.).

There are two general observations that can be reached from this data. First, there is an inconsistency in the approach of COI operations that directly affects their ability to meet their objectives. This inconsistency undermines overall potential impact of COIs as a viable institutional mechanism for post-

---

[13] Michelle Martin and Leticia Villarreal Sosa, Dominican University of River Forest Graduate School of Social Work, *An Empirical Analysis of United Nations Commissions of Inquiry: Toward the Development of a Standardized Methodology* 29 – 32 (2013).

conflict justice and the promotion of accountability in the face of violations of international humanitarian law (IHL) and international human rights law (IHRL). Second, the lack of universally accepted standards in methods of operation and investigation undermines the ultimate quality and reliability of individual COI findings, thereby undercutting their potential impact on the particular situation they are investigating.

One significant area in need of standardization is in the reporting of the COI's investigative methodology. The failure of most reports to provide a description of a COI's investigative methodology provides opportunities for political detractors to challenge its findings. This may, in part, be due to the failure of some missions to develop an investigative strategy prior to the commencement of operations.[14] *Ad hoc* investigative methods affect the quality of information gathered, as even investigators within the same mission will inevitably employ disparate tactics, leading to sometimes inaccurate information that, if revealed, will undermine the legitimacy of the mission.[15]

Even the articulation of a standard of proof has been inconsistent among UN COIs. In research conducted by the Académie de droit international humanitaire et droits humain à Genève, a variety of terms were found to have been used in different fact-finding mechanisms. These terms include "beyond reasonable doubt", "sufficient credible and reliable information", "sufficiently substantiated", "overwhelming evidence", "reasonable to assume", "serious and concurring evidence", "less than that expected by criminal trials", "evidence collected to demonstrate that a person may responsibly be suspected of committing a crime", "approach proper to judicial standards", "convincing proof", "leaves no doubt" and "requiring a reliable body of material."[16] In many cases, these terms are not adequately defined, making it impossible to determine the amount of evidence deemed adequate to reach these standards.

Further, it is difficult to conduct a cost-benefit analysis of international COIs because the reports do not provide specific information about their operating budgets, staffing and other important factors. However, some information can be pieced together on the operating budgets of UN-initiated COIs that is useful in determining whether they are effective mechanisms. For example, in his proposed program budget for the biennium 2012–2013,

---

[14] HPCR Working Paper 42, *supra* note 6.
[15] *Id.*
[16] Stephen Wilkinson, Académie de droit international humanitaire et droits humain à Genève, *Standards of Proof in International Humanitarian and Human Rights Fact-Finding and Inquiry Missions* 25 (2012).

the Secretary-General disclosed the following expenses for the HRC for fact-finding missions from 2006–2011:[17]

Activity	Cost (USD)
Independent Special Commission of Inquiry for Timor-Leste	937,451
High-level Commission of Inquiry on Lebanon	500,146
High-level mission concerning the situation of human rights in Darfur	206,197
Situation of human rights in Darfur	261,600
Total, 2006 – 2007	**1,905,394**
Situation of human rights in Myanmar and follow-up	46,700
Human rights situation in the Occupied Palestinian Territory: Follow-up to HRC resolutions S-1/1 and S-3/1	51,064
International Commission of Inquiry for Guinea	363,464
The grave violations of human rights in the Occupied Palestinian Territory (Goldstone Report)	369,092
Total, 2008 – 2009	**830,320**
Follow-up to the report of the United Nations Independent Fact-Finding Mission on the Gaza Conflict (Human Rights Council res 13/9)	214,988
Fact-Finding Mission on the Israeli attack on the humanitarian boat convoy (Human Rights Council res 14/1)	341,632
Follow-up to the report of the Independent International Fact-Finding Mission on the incident of the humanitarian flotilla (Human Rights Council resolution 15/1)	118,000
Commission of Inquiry on the Libyan Arab Jamahiriya (Human Rights Council res S-15/1)	635,292 (total) 2,141,934[18]
Commission of Inquiry on Côte d'Ivoire (Human Rights Council res 16/25)	365,056
Fact-Finding Mission to the Syrian Arab Republic (Human Rights Council res S-16/1)	236,340 (total) 1,461,407[19]
Commission of Inquiry on Libya 2 (estimated) (Human Rights Council res 17/17)	1,275,942
Commission of Inquiry on the Syrian Arab Republic (estimated) (Human Rights Council res S-17/1)	885,896
Total, 2010 – 2011	**4,073,146**
Commission of Inquiry on Libya 2 (estimated) (Human Rights Council res 17/17)	230,700
Commission of Inquiry on the Syrian Arab Republic (estimated) (Human Rights Council res S-17/1)	575,511
Total, 2012 – 2013 (as of 31 October 2011)	**806,211**

---

[17] U.N. Secretary-General, *Financing of unforeseen and extraordinary expenses arising from resolutions and decisions of the Human Rights Council: Rep. of the Secretary-General*, ¶17, U.N. Doc. A/66/558 (15 Nov. 2011).
[18] Estimated total for 2010–2011 budget and projected 2012 budget.
[19] Estimated total for 2010–2011 budget and projected 2012 budget.

Since none of the reports of these missions disclosed the number and type of staff required, it is difficult to assess the cost of the mission per person. Despite this, it is still possible to deduce some important observations from this information. Namely, that the costs of operating a COI, and the resources afforded to them, can vary as dramatically as their methods and outputs.

The largest amount ever spent on a COI was the COI on Libya, which cost over 2 million USD, but also took place over the course of a full year. However, per month, the COI on Libya cost approximately 178,495 USD. The High-Level COI on Lebanon cost approximately 250,073 USD per month.[20] The highest-costing COI per month was the International Commission of Inquiry on Guinea, which cost approximately 363,464 USD and conducted its investigation for 32 days.

The average monthly cost of the UN COIs whose budgets were published above, and for whom the timeframe of work is known, is 214,809 USD. Monthly costs of operation ranged from 73,819 USD[21] to 363,464 USD.[22] This range in costs is likely a result of differences in the number of staff, the equipment and facilities used, the number of in-country visits conducted and other issues that relate back to the *ad hoc* nature and diversity of methods for each COI.

The impact that Commissions of Inquiry create in a given situation is as varied as their structure and methods. Generally, the impact of a COI depends on factors such as whether the subject State consented to and cooperated with the investigation, whether the COI was considered legitimate by relevant parties, and who the mandating body was and to what extent it was able or willing to take some sort of action after the conclusion of the investigation.

In Commissions of Inquiry established by the UN Security Council, what occurs after the findings and recommendations of a commission are submitted is wholly dependent on political factors. Where the Security Council has an interest in pursuing a matter further, it does. For example, the Commission of Experts Established Pursuant to Security Council Resolution 780 (Yugoslavia Commission of Experts) has been widely accepted as very

---

[20] The COI on Lebanon was assigned an initial budget of 417,800 USD for its work. However, the total expenses, according to the Secretary-General's report amounted to 500,146. *See* Report of the HRC on its second special session, *Estimated administrative and programme budget implications of draft resolution A/HRC/S-2/L.1*, Annex I ¶ 2, U.N. Doc. A/HRC/S-2/2 (Aug. 17 2006).
[21] The grave violations of human rights in the Occupied Palestinian Territory (Goldstone Report).
[22] International Commission of Inquiry for Guinea.

effective, as it was the clear precursor to formal criminal prosecution in the former Yugoslavia. While the evidence compiled throughout the course of the Yugoslavia Commission was not admissible in criminal proceedings, its role in helping to "establish the location, character and scale of violations" inevitably led to the ICTY's indictment of 161 persons.[23]

Similarly, Independent Inquiry into the actions of the United Nations during the 1994 Genocide in Rwanda, established by the Security Council, led to the establishment of the ICTR. This, in turn, led to the prosecution of 72 individuals implicated in violations of international humanitarian law.[24] Additionally, the Security Council-established International Commission of Inquiry on Darfur led the Security Council to refer a situation to the International Criminal Court for the first time in its history.[25] This has led the ICC Prosecutor to initiate an investigation leading to a current four cases before the Pre-Trial Chamber, including one against Omar Al-Bashir, the current President of Sudan.[26]

By contrast, where the Security Council is stalled or chooses to "wait out" a situation, even the most egregious findings of a commission do not compel it to act. In the United Nations Commission on the Truth for El Salvador, which was also established by the Security Council, the mission provided findings establishing the commission, by all sides of the conflict, of extrajudicial killings, attacks on hospitals, enforced disappearances, massacres, death squad assassinations and abductions.[27] The report recommended a number of measures, including judicial reform and reparations for victims.[28] Unfortunately, however, the report's recommendations were rejected and not implemented by the government of El Salvador and armed forces.[29] The Security Council took no action toward El Salvador following reception of the report of the Commission.

Similarly, the International Commission of Inquiry mandated to establish the facts and circumstances of the events of 28 September 2009 in Guinea, established by the UN Secretary-General and supported by the Security Council, has been unable to lead to decisive action by the government of Guinea or the United Nations. The Commission was mandated to investigate events that occurred on 28 September 2009 and related events

---

[23] Wilkinson 27, *supra* note 14.
[24] International Criminal Tribunal for Rwanda, http://www.unictr.org/AboutICTR/GeneralInformation/tabid/101/Default.aspx.
[25] Wilkinson 31, *supra* note 14.
[26] *Id.*
[27] *Id.* at 28.
[28] *Id.*
[29] *Id.* at 29.

regarding alleged massacres and rapes in Conakry stadium in Guinea. The Commission found that serious human rights violations occurred, including rape, sexual mutilation, torture, arbitrary detention, and killings and executions, listed publicly the names of individuals believed to have been involved, and made a number of recommendations including asking the government to ensure that victims were compensated and protected.[30] Since then, little action has been taken by the Security Council, and the matter has been under "preliminary analysis" by the ICC Prosecutor since October 2009.[31] Although government representatives of Guinea indicated willingness to implement the Commission's recommendations, no decisive action has been taken by the national government either.[32]

Commissions of Inquiry mandated by the HRC are even less effective on the whole, mainly because the HRC is not always able to elicit the requisite consent or cooperation by the subject State necessary to effect change, nor can it do anything beyond providing recommendations for other UN bodies to take action. For example, the HRC-established Fact-Finding Mission on the Gaza Conflict found a number of violations of international human rights law and international humanitarian law during Israeli military operations in Gaza between 19 June 2008 and 31 July 2009, particularly with respect to Israel's blockade on Gaza, the targeting of civilians and civilian targets, and the conditions of detention for Palestinian prisoners. As a result of the report, Israel conducted 400 command investigations in relation to Operation Cast Lead and 52 criminal investigations.[33] However, this has led to a total of only three prosecutions. The Israeli government has also been accused of partiality, and the level of victim participation and their treatment throughout the processes has been criticized.[34] Sentencing has also been critiqued. For example, two soldiers who forced a boy to search bags suspected of being booby-trapped were only demoted and received suspended sentences.[35]

Additionally, the international community has been unable to take any effective action with respect to events currently unfolding in Syria, even after the HRC-established Independent Commission of Inquiry on the Syrian Arab Republic has found serious violations of IHL and IHRL.[36]

---

[30] *Id.* at 34.
[31] *Id.* at 35.
[32] *Id.*
[33] *Id.* at 33.
[34] *Id.*
[35] *Id.*
[36] Independent International Commission of Inquiry on the Syrian Arab Republic, *Report to the Human Rights Council pursuant to resolutions S/17-1 (2011), 19/22 (2012)*

Indeed, each report of the COI on Syria indicates an escalation of casualties, refugees and the disregard for civilians and civilian infrastructure, yet the international community has remained stalled on taking any decisive action due to backroom politics and public stalemates between members of the UN Security Council.

Thus, many factors contribute to whether and to what extent a COI has an impact on a particular situation on the ground. What is apparent, however, is that the UN system must develop better and more centralized coordination procedures and methods, and that follow up procedures are established in each case to ensure the implementation of recommendations following the conclusion of a mission.

Special Procedures

The UN Special Procedures system is a mechanism mandated by the HRC for the purpose of reporting specific human rights issues, typically organized by theme or geography. The purpose of reporting mechanisms such as Special Procedures is to mitigate human rights violations by facilitating an advisory relationship with the State in question and to examine specific incidents of alleged violations.[37] Thus, in assessing whether this particular mechanism is effective, one must evaluate the impact that Special Procedures have had on the actual policies and practices of States. Special Procedures also serve to inform the HRC of trends and incidents specific to their mandates. Toward this end, an assessment must include whether the reports and studies conducted by Special Procedures mandate holders have actually impacted upon the policies and actions of the international community as a whole when taken with respect to a particular issue or geographic area. Unfortunately, oftentimes when assessing the effectiveness of Special Procedures, the evaluation stops at whether reports and studies are generated, and, if so, how many.

---

and 21/26 (2012), U.N. Doc. A/HRC/22/59 (Feb. 5, 2013); Independent International Commission of Inquiry on the Syrian Arab Republic, *Periodic Update to the Human Rights Council pursuant to resolutions S/17-1 (2011), 19/22 (2012) and 21/26 (2012)* (Dec. 20, 2012); Independent International Commission of Inquiry on the Syrian Arab Republic, *Periodic Update to the Human Rights Council pursuant to resolutions S/17-1 (2011) and 19/22 (2012)* (May 24, 2012).

[37] HPCR Working Paper 10, *supra* note 6.

Methods and Costs of Special Procedures

Currently, there are a total of 35 thematic mandates and 10 country-specific mandates. Special Procedures mandates, whether thematic or geographic, receive a total of 13 million USD per year, less than 7 percent of the UN budget allocated to human rights work.[38] This lack of resources for Special Procedures requires mandate holders to seek funding from outside sources, which often calls into question the quality and independence of their work.

Since the HRC is entirely comprised of and controlled by Member States, Special Procedures are politicized with respect to their establishment and the selection of mandate holders. The HRC determines what thematic issues or country-specific mandates to establish, and specifically constructs the scope of each mandate. This is an inevitably political process. Moreover, although mandate holders may be nominated by governments, NGOs, other UN bodies or individuals, the final list of candidates is developed by the HRC President, the approval of which is left only to HRC members. There is also little consideration for overlapping work within the various human rights mechanisms, especially with respect to existing mechanisms under the treaty body system. For example, Special Procedures can be used to report on the implementation of COI recommendations, be they international or national in character. If done systematically, it could potentially be an effective, already-existing mechanism to monitor and report on the actions of States and the international community following a COI.

Special Procedures are unique in that they are long-term mechanisms that report human rights situations to the HRC, and at the same time are able to provide recommendations to governments regarding a given situation. Through Special Procedures, the HRC is also able to monitor developments in the globe as a whole, since rapporteurs are often mandated to perform country visits to obtain first-hand information about developments in particular countries (through country-specific mandates) or globally (through thematic mandates).

Thematic mandates for special procedures vary, but often include a mandate to perform country visits, engage in dialogue with governments, respond to communications concerning alleged human rights violations related to the mandate, perform a study related to the theme of the mandate, and submit an annual report to the HRC. Country-specific mandates may include a technical assistance mandate, which involves aiding the

---

[38] Human rights work receives $193 million, less than 3 percent of the UN budget. *See* Ted Piccone, *Catalysts for Change: How the UN's Independent Experts Promote Human Rights* 124 (2012).

government in implementing recommendations that have been put forth by another body, in addition to engaging in dialogue with governments and apprising the international community of developments. Alternatively, a country-specific mandate may incorporate a monitoring mandate which involves communicating with governments, responding to communications concerning alleged human rights violations, and apprising the international community of developments. Annual reports are submitted by all Special Procedures and often contain recommendations provided by the rapporteur or independent expert that are designed to help States address human rights issues relevant to the mandate.

However, States are under no international obligation to apply recommendations put forth by a mandate holder. In fact, the HRC's Universal Periodic Review (UPR) mechanism, which takes into account information contained in the reports of Special Procedures, indicates that, for the most part, recommendations by rapporteurs are ignored. Additionally, research conducted by the Brookings Institute indicates that communications sent to governments between 2004 and 2008 through Special Procedures thematic mandates were largely disregarded. Nearly 59 percent of communications to governments for all thematic mandates received no response or immaterial responses, 21 percent were rejected without substantiation, and 14.8 percent were "responsive but incomplete"[39, 40] Only 3.5 percent of communications indicated that steps were taken to address an alleged violation.[41]

Country-specific mandates fare no better. A review of the HRC's current ten country-specific mandates indicates little progress with respect to the implementation of recommendations, with the exception of the Special Rapporteur on the situation of human rights in Myanmar. There, the Special Rapporteur has acknowledged steps taken by the government that have had a "positive impact on the human rights situation in Myanmar," but has also cautioned against the persistence of "many serious human rights issues encompassing the broad range of civil, political, economic, social and cultural rights" that must be addressed.[42] Recently Israel became the first nation to boycott the UPR mechanism altogether, expressing

---

[39] *Id.* at 176. Responsive but Incomplete is defined in the researcher's methodology as when the "government responds to and addresses the violation alleged by the special procedures communication, but the reply either does not fully respond to the allegations or, for a communication referencing multiple individuals or violations, the government reply responds only with regard to some. Also included are responses that indicate that an investigation has been ordered or commenced but is not yet concluded."

[40] *Id.* at 36.

[41] *Id.*

[42] Special Rapporteur on the situation of Human Rights in Myanmar, *Progress Report*, U.N. Doc. A/HRC/19/67, ¶ 84 (Mar. 7 2012) (by Philip Alston).

frustration over the HRC's consistent attention to human rights conditions in the Occupied Palestinian Territories, which it perceives to be biased and politically motivated.[43] Moreover, mandate holders are often unable to conduct country visits to certain countries. For example, the governments of Sudan, Israel, Syria and North Korea have not permitted visits by mandate holders, leaving mandate holders to travel to neighboring states and find other avenues of obtaining information. This inevitably impedes upon the quality and impact of their work.

Treaty Bodies

When discussing the treaty body system, there are generally two misguided presumptions that form the basis for the discussions regarding reforming the methods of the system. The first is that the treaty body system is a mechanism designed to facilitate enforcement of human rights treaties. The second is that the system is accidentally inefficient.

The treaty body system is not an enforcement mechanism in the traditional sense. Rather, the committees that are formed are mandated to monitor the implementation of their respective treaties. Being committees elected by State Parties, comprised significantly of government officials, and having no power to issue binding observations or recommendations, these treaty bodies act more as peer reviewers than as enforcers. This is not to undercut their potential influence in bettering the condition of human rights throughout the world. Political mechanisms can be as effective as legal ones. But if an assessment is to be conducted as to their efficacy, it is only fair that they be judged on the basis of what they are designed to do, and nothing more. Thus, in evaluating the efficacy of the treaty body system, one must determine whether the methods and activities of the various treaty bodies has adequately encouraged and supported State Parties in the implementation of their respective treaty obligations.

This leads to the second misguided presumption: that the system is accidentally inefficient. Very often the discussion is framed around the notion that the treaty body system is ill-equipped to carry out its mandated work, and that these inadequacies were somehow unforeseen or accidental consequences of poor structure and organization. The fact is that the treaty body system is weak because it was designed that way. Treaty bodies, and the UN staff designated to provide support to them, are significantly under-

---

[43] Nick Cumming-Bruce, *Israel Skips U.N. Review on Rights, a New Move*, N.Y. Times, Jan. 29, 2013, available at http://www.nytimes.com/2013/01/30/world/europe/israel-to-boycott-un-human-rights-review.html?hp&_r=1&.

resourced, while at the same time the size, scope and number of treaty bodies continues to expand disproportionately. Significant resources are thus paid to the receipt and review of periodic reports by State parties, and not enough resources are expended on ensuring the quality of recommendations and or to monitor their implementation or follow up. It is a system designed to fail so that State Parties have the least amount of enforcement in order to ensure that they will have the widest latitude of action and the least exposure to condemnation or embarrassment.[44]

Methods and Costs of the Treaty Body System

To understand and assess the effectiveness of the treaty body system, one must first consider that the objective of the system is not to act as an enforcer in the traditional sense of the term, but more as a peer reviewer, and when necessary a mediator, in order to facilitate compliance with the various human rights treaties. Each treaty body establishes an international committee of experts to monitor the implementation of the provisions of its respective treaty.[45] Currently, there are ten different treaty bodies.[46] All treaty bodies, with the exception of the SPT, are mandated to receive and review periodic reports from State Parties and receive communications for individuals regarding allegations of rights violations by a State Party.[47] Of these ten treaty bodies, six are given the authority to conduct country inquiries and/or visits, although of the six, two have yet to enter into force.[48] Some have established follow up procedures that require State Parties to submit additional reports regarding the implementation of recommendations within one or two years after their issuance.[49] Each of

---

[44] Bassiouni, *supra* note 3.
[45] Navanethem Pillay, United Nations Office of the High Commissioner for Human Rights, *Strengthening the United Nations human rights treaty body system, Rep. of the United Nations High Commissioner for Human Rights*, at 16 (2012) (hereinafter "OHCHR 2012 Report").
[46] These treaty bodies are: Human Rights Committee (CCPR); Committee on Economic, Social and Cultural Rights (CESCR); Committee on the Elimination of Racial Discrimination (CERD); Committee on the Elimination of Discrimination Against Women (CEDAW); Committee Against Torture (CAT); Committee on the Rights of the Child (CRC); Committee on Migrant Workers (CMW); Committee on the Rights of Persons with Disabilities (CRPD); Committee on Enforced Disappearance (CED); and the recently-established Subcommittee on the Prevention of Torture (SPT).
[47] OHCHR 2012 Report at 16, *supra* note 42.
[48] These treaty bodies are: SPT, CED, CAT, CRPD, CEDAW and the ICESR.
[49] Michael O'Flaherty and Pei-Lun Tsai, *Periodic Reporting: the Backbone of the UN Treaty Body Review Procedures*, in NEW CHALLENGES FOR THE UN HUMAN RIGHTS MACHINERY, 40 (M. Cherif Bassiouni & William Schabas eds., 2011).

these treaty bodies functions completely independently of the others. This leads to different methods of operation and composition, and inevitably, to different products. Moreover, there is no systematic collaboration between these treaty bodies and Special Procedures that have parallel thematic mandates.

The problems typically identified with the treaty body system are: overdue reports by State Parties; backlogs in the review of State Party reports and individual complaints; growing costs of translation and documentation; decreased capacity of State Parties to report; overlapping and cumbersome reporting requirements between the various treaty bodies; and insufficient financial and human resources capacity of the OHCHR. Moreover, these problems tend to feed into one another, reinforcing and further rooting inefficiencies imbedded into the system. As noted by the current High Commissioner for Human Rights, "When a treaty mechanism can only function by tolerating an 84 [percent] rate of non-compliance in reporting, serious measures are in order."[50]

Another often-cited criticism of treaty bodies is that there is a lack of coordination between them and Special Procedures with overlapping thematic mandates. Of the 35 existing thematic mandates for Special Procedures, 24 have clear overlap with at least one treaty body.[51] For this reason, one of the recommendations put forth by the OHCHR has been to systematize the interaction between treaty bodies and Special Procedures, such as by suggesting to Special Procedures mandate holders to undertake a country visit to a State Party when the State Party requires support in implementing recommendations, fails to implement recommendations, or when repeated violations are committed.[52]

---

[50] OHCHR 2012 Report at 28, *supra* note 42.
[51] These are: 1) Adequate housing as a component of right to an adequate standard of living and the right to non-discrimination in this context; 2) Sale of children, child prostitution and child pornography; 3) Right to education; 4) Extreme poverty and human rights; 5) Effects of foreign debt and other related international financial obligations of States on the full enjoyment of human rights, particularly economic, social and cultural rights; 6) Situation of human rights defender; 7) Rights of indigenous peoples; 8) Human rights of migrants; 9) Trafficking in persons, especially women and children; 10) Violence against women, its causes and consequences; 11) Promotion and protection of human rights while countering terrorism; 12) Extrajudicial, summary or arbitrary executions; 13) Contemporary forms of racism; 14) Contemporary forms of slavery including its causes and consequences; 15) Cultural rights; 16) Right to freedom of peaceful assembly and association; 17) Minority issues; 18) Freedom of religion or belief; 19) Freedom of opinion and expression; 20) Special rapporteur on torture; 21) Discrimination against women in law and in practice; 22) Enforced or involuntary disappearance; 23) People of African descent; 24) Arbitrary detention.
[52] OHCHR 2012 Report at 81, *supra* note 42.

The OHCHR, through the Human Rights Treaties Division (HRTD), provides staff support for the work of the treaty bodies. However, as the treaty body system has expanded, doubling in size since 2004, the provision of financial resources to the OHCHR has lagged behind.[53]

For the 2010–2011 biennium, the annual budget for treaty bodies was 39.3 million USD.[54] Funding for treaty bodies is generally drawn from two sources, the regular budget (74.3%) and voluntary contributions from donors (25.7 percent).[55, 56] In 2010, expenses were divided between staff support from the HRTD (71.5%), and travel expenses for treaty body experts (28.5 percent).[57] Treaty bodies rely heavily on the Secretariat, through the HRTD, for support in carrying out their work, creating a strain on its human and logistical resources. In fact, in the span of less than five years, the number of treaty bodies increased from five to 10, increasing the number of experts requesting support from the Secretariat from 74 to 172.[58] This strain has resulted in a lower quality of work for Secretariat staff performing services for these treaty bodies. Although the budget allocated for treaty body work, specifically to the HRTD, has nearly tripled over the last ten years, it has been regarded as insufficient to keep up with the increasing work load caused by the increase of treaty body experts and activities.[59] For this reason, the OHCHR has reported a need for an additional 14 professional staff members for the HRTD in order to sustain the current work load of the various treaty bodies.[60]

The committee members of the various treaty bodies receive no salary for their work. However, the cost of travel and stay for committee members to participate in sessions amounts to 31 percent ($12.1 million) of the budget

---

[53] *Id.* at 17, 26.
[54] *Id.*
[55] Office of the High Commissioner for Human Rights, Background paper for the Consultation with States Parties, Sion, Switzerland, *Resources in support of the human rights treaty body system* 2 (May 11, 2011) (hereinafter "OHCHR-Sion Resources Report").
[56] In a later report submitted by the OHCHR, this figure was represented as 76 percent from the regular budget ($29.7 million) and 23 percent from voluntary contributions ($9.6 million) for the period 2010–2011. See OHCHR 2012 Report 26, *supra* note 42.
[57] OHCHR-Sion Resources Report 1, *supra* note 52.
[58] OHCHR 2012 Report 17, 26, *supra* note 42.
[59] Office of the High Commissioner for Human Rights, Background paper prepared by the OHCHR for the Consultation with States Parties, Sion, Switzerland, *State parties' reporting procedures under international human rights treaties: Requirements and implications of the ongoing growth of the treaty body system on the periodic reporting procedures, documentation and meeting time* (May 12–13, 2011) (hereinafter "OHCHR-Sion Background Paper").
[60] OHCHR-Sion Resources Report 7, *supra* note 52.

allocated for the work of treaty bodies.[61] This figure is nearly triple the budget allocated for this purpose in 2000–2001, mainly due to the increase in experts from 74 in 2000 to 172 in 2011.[62]

The challenges faced by the inadequate resources allocated to treaty body work raise questions about the efficiency of the system's structure and methods. The abundance of duplicative work between mechanisms and overemphasis on bureaucratized report production and processing renders treaty bodies slow, and consequently ineffective. At the same time, this mechanism has created a steadily increasing burden on the OHCHR, both in terms of finances and personnel.

With the exception of only the SPT, the principal mandate of treaty bodies is to review the periodic reports of State parties. Additional activities that comprise the essence of mandated core work for treaty bodies varies, but may include receiving inter-State complaints, receiving individual complaints, and issuing general recommendations. In the case of the CERD, it is also mandated to engage in early warning or urgent action procedures, which allows a working group of five members to request a State party provide explanations when reliable information is presented that indicates that the State party has or is engaged in serious, massive and persistent violations of the treaty concerned.[63] This procedure typically results in the CERD issuing general public statements regarding a particular situation.[64]

Treaty bodies are plagued with an additional two persistent problems: on the one hand, they are unable to get State parties to comply with their reporting obligations on time, resulting in submission delays of up to 10 years; on the other hand they are unable to review all of the reports submitted in a timely manner, resulting in a backlog in reviewing reports that are submitted to them. These backlogs affect not only the timeliness of the reviews conducted by treaty bodies, but also discredits their perceived authority by State parties, making them outdated and ineffective.

That the procedures for treaty bodies are slow is no accident. The procedures were designed in such a fashion to allow States the least amount of intervention and oversight possible. Currently, most treaty bodies meet

---

[61] OHCHR 2012 Report 26, *supra* note 42.
[62] *Id.*
[63] While the procedure is not specifically indicated in the Convention, the procedure was developed under article 9(1)(b), which entitles the Committee to request additional information from reporting State parties.
[64] For example, during events in the MENA region that have come to be referred to as the Arab Spring, the CERD limited itself to issuing statements about events in Libya and Syria. Report of the Committee on the Elimination of Racial Discrimination, U.N. Doc. A/66/18 ¶ 20, GAOR, 66th Sess. Supp. No. 18 (2011).

for sessions two or three times per year for a period of two to three weeks at a time. During these sessions, committees review reports submitted by State parties, address individual communications and issue general recommendations. Within most treaty bodies, there is a mechanism that allows a State party to bring a complaint against a State, but only under the CERD is this procedure obligatory before the complaining State party can pursue other avenues.[65]

Treaties have no doubt had an impact in shaping the understanding and condition of human rights throughout the world. However, the question remains as to whether the treaty body system is effective at fostering the implementation of human rights treaties, especially at its current costs. Studies have shown that treaties have the greatest impact where they have been made a part of domestic law, and are less effective when enforced through treaty bodies.[66] This is in part due to the fact that the treaty body system took a number of years to develop, and still faces a number of obstacles (i.e. backlogs, overlaps, vagueness in findings, etc.).[67] It is also in part due to the fact that there are no actual enforcement powers given to treaty bodies.[68] In fact, even where recommendations are timely and specific, they are routinely ignored when it is politically convenient.[69]

Nevertheless, close to $40 million is expended for the treaty body budget, and even with this budget, it cannot actually maintain its own workload. Proposals to reform the treaty body system tend to focus on increasing the efficiency of the reporting process by reducing backlogs and

---

[65] To take but one example, see the recent case of *Georgia v. Russia* in the International Court of Justice (ICJ), in which the Court rejected the case brought by Georgia against Russia, for alleged violation of the Convention of the Elimination of all forms of Racial Discrimination, on the basis that the Court lacked jurisdiction since Georgia failed to raise the issue first with the respective Committee (CERD) before bringing the case to the ICJ. However, despite appearing before the Committee subsequent to this, Georgia did not ask CERD to consider the dispute with Russia that prompted it to file its case before the ICJ. For further details see: ICJ, Application of the International Convention on the Elimination of All Forms of Racial Discrimination (*Georgia v. Russian Federation*), Preliminary Objections, No. 2011/9, 11 April 2011, available at: www.icj-cij.org/docket/files/140/16396.pdf. See also proceedings of the 79th session of the CERD, 8 August – 2 September 2011 (4th to 5th periodic report of Georgia) available at: www2.ohchr.org/English/bodies/cerd/cerds79.htm.

[66] Bassiouni, *supra* note 3; Christof Heyns and Frans Viljoen, *The Impact of the United Nations Human Rights Treaties on the Domestic Level* 5 (2002).

[67] Heyns & Viljoen 6, *supra* note 63.

[68] Felice D. Gaer, *Implementing Treaty Body Recommendations: Establishing Better Follow-Up Procedures*, in NEW CHALLENGES FOR THE UN HUMAN RIGHTS MACHINERY (M. Cherif Bassiouni and William A. Schabas eds., 2011).

[69] Heyns & Viljoen 6, *supra* note 63.

overdue reports.[70] This is because once recommendations have been issued and are in the hands of the State party, there is little that can actually be done to enforce the recommendations. There is no quantifiable consequence for State parties that do not properly implement their treaty obligations. However, rather than acknowledging this and therefore strengthening the system by focusing on strengthening follow up procedures or coordinating with other UN mechanisms not so confined by the politically conservative terms of a treaty, far too much focus is paid to the reporting process, lending to the image that the review of a report is an end in and of itself.

DE-FACTO FACT-FINDING MISSIONS UNDERTAKEN BY THE UN DEPARTMENT OF PEACEKEEPING OPERATIONS (DPKO)

Since 1948, there have been a total of 67 peacekeeping operations.[71] Currently, the DPKO directs 15 peace operations: 14 peacekeeping operations[72] and one political mission.[73] Rule of Law work has been done through the Department of Peacekeeping Operations (DPKO) since the 1990s. Recently, even greater emphasis has been placed on the role of the DPKO in rule of law work as a key component of peacekeeping, conflict resolution and peace-building.[74] This work *de facto* involves fact-finding as a means of assessing the needs of a given post-conflict justice situation (although the findings are generally not made public). This comes as a part of the Secretariat's strategic assessment tool to better advise the Security

---

[70] OHCHR 2012 Report, *supra* note 42.
[71] Fact Sheet, United Nations Department of Peacekeeping Operations (Dec. 31, 2012) (hereinafter "DPKO Factsheet").
[72] These peacekeeping operations are: 1) UN Truce Supervision Organization (UNTSO); 2) UN Military Observer Group in India and Pakistan (UNMOGIP); 3) UN Peacekeeping Force in Cyprus (UNFICYP); 4) UN Disengagement Observer Force (UNDOF); 5) UN Interim Force in Lebanon (UNIFIL); 6) UN Mission for the Referendum in Western Sahara (MINURSO); 7) UN Interim Administration Mission in Kosovo (UNMIK); 8) United Nations Mission in Liberia (UNMIL); 9) United Nations Operations in Côte d'Ivoire; 10) United Nations Stabilization Mission in Haiti (MINUSTAH); 11) African Union-United Nations Hybrid Operation in Darfur (UNAMID); 12) United Nations Organization Stabilization Mission in the Democratic Republic of the Congo (MONUSCO); 13) United Nations Interim Security Force for Abyei (UNISFA); 14) United Nations Mission in the Republic of South Sudan (UNMISS).
[73] The political mission directed by the UNDPKO is the United Nations Assistance Mission in Afghanistan (UNAMA).
[74] G.A. Res. 67/1, ¶ 18, U.N. Doc. A/RES/67/1 (Nov. 30, 2012).

Council and UN Member States on the conditions and risks of a particular crisis, as well as the range of potential responses.[75]

Assessments can involve providing the general context of a given situation, but may also include investigating allegations of IHL and IHRL violations. Assessment reports can also inform the DPKO of how to shape the operation itself.[76] As these reports are generally not made public, it is difficult to conduct an assessment of their methods of operation and investigation. However, recent notes have been made regarding the need to address problems with DPKO operations that do provide some insight into the challenges faced. For example, each mission is created in the same *ad hoc* manner characterized by other UN fact-finding mechanisms.[77] Missions are built "from scratch" and function with their own administrative, logistical and budgetary operations.[78] This inevitably creates the same kind of overlap, loss of time and financial loss as other UN mechanisms plagued with the same problem.[79]

With fact-finding functions that directly relate to observer and monitoring missions (such as in the case of Syria in recent years) no information is available as to where these reports end up or what their contents are, but their substance or summary is shared with the UN Secretary-General and the UN Security Council. This is arguably the most highly politicized and secretive aspect of UN fact-finding. Due to political reasons, this data is not used for other UN mechanisms and is not made public. They are not shared with the International Criminal Court (ICC), even in situations where the UN Security Council has referred the situation. One example of this is the UN peacekeeping forces operating in the former Yugoslavia, including what was then called CivPol, never having reported their findings on IHL or IHRL violations to the Commission of Experts or the ICTY.

In the context of peacekeeping operations which do not mandate fact-finding, assessments are necessary in order to make tactical decisions on the deployment of forces or risk-assessment once forces are on the ground. In the situation in Darfur, for example, the operations were essentially belonging to

---

[75] United Nations Department of Peacekeeping Operations Non-Paper, *A New Partnership Agenda: Charting a New Horizon for UN Peacekeeping* (July 2009) (hereinafter "DPKO non-paper".
[76] U.N. Secretary-General, *Third annual progress report on the implementation of the global field support strategy: Rep. of the Secretary-General*, ¶ 40, U.N. Doc. A/67/633 (Dec. 12, 2012) (hereinafter "UNSG Report").
[77] DPKO non-paper 4, *supra* note 72.
[78] UNSG Report ¶ 4, *supra* note 73.
[79] *Id.* ¶ 6.

ECOWAS and under the supervision of the DPKO. The DPKO is believed to have collected extensive data on IHL and IHRL violations committed by the government and paramilitary units supported by the government, namely the *Janjawid*, but the relevant information was not provided to the ICC, which has the jurisdiction to investigate and prosecute crimes committed in Darfur as a result of the Security Council referral.

The DPKO operates on an annual budget of 7.33 billion, with outstanding contributions amounting to approximately 1.33 billion.[80] It currently oversees a staff of 112,735 individuals comprising of troops, military observers, police, international civilians, local civilians and UN volunteers.[81] However, as stated above, it is impossible to assess the reliability and effectiveness of the different DPKO fact-finding operations and therefore impossible to compare them. The disparity in methods is also likely to result in different decision-making by the Secretary-General and the Security Council.[82]

National Fact-Finding Bodies

Several national fact-finding bodies have been created with an investigative mandate as a response to allegations of violations of international human rights and humanitarian law. Perhaps even more than their international counterparts, because each situation is sui generis, the format, size and scope of a national fact-finding body can vary depending upon its specific objectives. These variances are further highlighted by different national legal and political systems, interests, needs and resources. Some bodies operate with multi-million dollar annual budgets over the span of several years, while others operate on minimal budgets over the course of a few months. National fact-finding bodies may be purely investigatory, quasi-judicial, or have truth and reconciliation components attached. In any of these cases, however, the first necessary step is always the process of fact-finding. A national fact-finding body has a potentially significant impact on the ground because of the State's direct investment in the mechanism, but if not conducted optimally can potentially delay accountability measures and prolong human rights violations that are ongoing or systematic.

The United States Institute of Peace has compiled information on 33 truth commissions and 11 smaller-scaled national COIs established up to

---

[80] DPKO Factsheet, *supra* note 68.
[81] Id.
[82] This work cannot be undertaken within the present framework of our project because of its scope and depth. A partner will have to be found to undertake this work.

March 2011, although its list is not exhaustive.[83] Of 23 national commissions whose budgets are available, the average monthly costs of operations is 318,160 USD, although the range for these figures is rather wide, ranging from less than 20,000 per month to over 1 million per month.[84] This disparity is a natural consequence of the different resources, objectives and interests at play in each nation that decides to establish a fact-finding body. There is no comprehensive assessment of the fact-finding methods of nationally established fact-finding bodies, but as the disparity in their resources, objectives, scopes, spans and outcomes suggests, there is likely much diversity in this respect as well.

One of the largest national fact-finding bodies established was the South African Truth and Reconciliation Commission (TRC), which operated between 1995 until 2002. The South African TRC's mandate was to investigate gross violations of human rights, which was defined as "the killing, abduction, torture or severe ill-treatment of any person," or the "conspiracy, incitement, instigation, or command" of such acts "which emanated from conflicts of the past … within or outside of the Republic, and the commission of which was advised, planned, directed, commanded or ordered by any person acting with a political motive."[85] The TRC worked over a period of six years, conducting investigations and public hearings, and operated on a total budget of 55 million USD, 300 staff members and a number of offices throughout the country.[86]

Resource-wise, the South African TRC is second only to the Truth and Reconciliation Commission of Canada. With a projected budget of 60 million USD for a five year operation, the Canadian TRC is mandated to investigate government-funded, church-run schools set up to eliminate parental involvement in the intellectual, cultural, and spiritual development of Aboriginal children from 1874 until 1996.[87] The work of the Canadian TRC is still ongoing.

Insofar as national fact-finding bodies can be seen as part of the system of indirect enforcement of international human rights and humanitarian law, strengthening their functioning worldwide is important in promoting

---

[83] United States Institute of Peace, Truth Commission Digital Collection, http://www.usip.org/publications/truth-commission-digital-collection.
[84] These figures were determined by calculating budgets presented in Appendix 2 of Priscilla B. Hayner, UNSPEAKABLE TRUTHS: TRANSITIONAL JUSTICE AND THE CHALLENGE OF TRUTH COMMISSIONS 274, Routledge (2011), along with the Final Audit of the Bahrain Independent Commission of Inquiry http://www.bici.org.bh/BICIfinalaudit.pdf.
[85] HAYNER 266, *supra* note 82.
[86] *Id.* 269.
[87] Truth and Reconciliation Commission of Canada, http://www.trc.ca/websites/trcinstitution/index.php?p=4.

the overall enforcement system of human rights. Indirect enforcement mechanisms are vital components of enforcement for the simple reason that direct enforcement mechanisms (i.e. international courts and tribunals and even international fact-finding bodies) are not designed to be exhaustive enough to address all human rights and humanitarian law violations everywhere. National implementation of human rights and humanitarian law, as reflected by the establishment of national fact-finding bodies, in addition to other forms of implementation such as domestic legislation and prosecution, is an important development in the enforcement of human rights and humanitarian law because it promotes the recognition of and adherence to these laws at the local level.

A national fact-finding body should therefore be pursued before the establishment of an international fact-finding body.[88] A national fact-finding body's "proximity to the affected population often adds to the legitimacy and potential impact of a commission of inquiry."[89] A fact-finding body established by a national government is significant because, whereas the relationship between international fact-finding mechanisms is between the mandating body and the state(s) in question, national fact-finding bodies are a reflection of the relationship between the state and the citizen, and particularly the victim. A state establishing a national fact-finding body creates an expectation and obligation on itself to address the issues that are the subject of the investigation. In these cases, it is the state itself that opens the door to inquiry into its actions on a particular subject, and to further criticism if it fails to adequately respond to the findings of the inquiry.

The major problems with national fact-finding bodies emerge when the mission fails to adhere to the most basic standards accepted for such missions. These basic standards include: maintaining the mission's independence, impartiality and neutrality; providing the mission with access to important evidence; effectively protecting the mission and the witnesses or victims who come forward; providing the mission with adequate funding and sufficient resources; and making the mission's results available to the

---

[88] Special Rapporteur on torture and other cruel, inhuman or degrading treatment of punishment, *Report of the Special Rapporteur on torture and other cruel, inhuman or degrading treatment or punishment* ¶ 59, U.N. Doc. A/HRC/19/61 (18 Jan 2012) (by Juan Méndez).

[89] Special Rapporteur on torture and other cruel, inhuman or degrading treatment of punishment, *Report of the Special Rapporteur on torture and other cruel, inhuman or degrading treatment or punishment* ¶ 59, U.N. Doc. A/HRC/19/61 (18 Jan 2012) (by Juan Méndez).

public.[90] Additionally, merely establishing a national fact-finding body does not relieve a state of its duty to enforce legislation criminalizing specific acts, prosecute offenders, provide redress and reparations for victims, or take other steps in accordance with their international obligations.[91]

For example, issues of whether alleged perpetrators should be given amnesty in exchange for their testimony before a national fact-finding body often arise. While most fact-finding bodies do not have formal or informal policies with respect to granting amnesties, some notable bodies did operate in this context. The South African TRC, for example, considered amnesty for "acts, omissions and offences associated with political objectives and committed in the course of the conflicts of the past."[92] Commissions in Sierra Leone and Ghana also operated where amnesty for perpetrators applied, and in the case of El Salvador, blanket amnesty was passed after the Commission's report was released.[93] Amnesty policies often lead to discontent among members of the public who believe that perpetrators of human rights violations should not be absolved of their past crimes simply for their participation in public hearings. Additionally, amnesty laws may prevent the prosecution of those responsible for war crimes, genocide, crimes against humanity and other gross violations of human rights, which may be required under a State's obligations under international law.[94]

Additionally, where a mission's independence is in question, its findings will not be considered legitimate by all relevant parties. An example of a commission's failure to remain independent is in one of the COIs established in Sri Lanka in November of 2006. The mission was criticized for having serious conflicts of interest, including the use of the Attorney-General's Department in providing legal counsel to the commission, at the same time that it was acting as the chief legal adviser to the Government of Sri Lanka.[95] The mission's findings were criticized by an International Independent Group of Eminent Persons established by the government to monitor the work of the commission and report on its conformity with international

---

[90] American Society of International Law, *Panel on Commissions of Inquiry into Armed Conflict, Breaches of the Laws of War, and Human Rights Abuses: Process, Standards, and Lessons Learned*, 105 Am. Soc'y of Int'l L. Proc. 81, 83 (2011).
[91] Méndez ¶ 24, *supra* note 86.
[92] Hayner 27, *supra* note 82.
[93] *Id.* at 105.
[94] Méndez ¶ 56, *supra* note 86.
[95] Special Rapporteur on extrajudicial, summary or arbitrary executions, *Promotion and protection of all human rights, civil, political, economic, social and cultural rights, including the right to development: Rep. of the Special Rapporteur on extrajudicial, summary or arbitrary executions* ¶34, U.N. Doc. A/HRC/8/3 (2 May 2008) (by Philip Alston).

standards.⁹⁶ Where staff, witnesses and victims are not provided with adequate protection, an environment of impunity is established and proper investigations cannot be carried out. This was the case in Colombia in 1989, when a commission was established to investigate a massacre that occurred in October of 1987. After 12 of the 15 members of the commission were killed on 18 January 1989, and proper protection was not provided to remaining members of the mission or to witnesses, the investigation could not adequately be carried out.⁹⁷

On the contrary, where a national COI is able to meet basic international standards, they can have an important role in combating impunity, resolving internal conflict and preventing future violations. For example, after extrajudicial killings had been committed by Canadian soldiers in Somalia, the government of Canada established a COI to determine what institutional deficiencies had allowed the events to occur.⁹⁸ Through the findings of the commission, the Canadian government was able to strengthen its institutional capacity to prevent future abuses.⁹⁹ In Brazil, a COI established to investigate the deaths of detainees in police custody led government officials to support the provision of reparations for the families of the victims.¹⁰⁰ In Bahrain, the establishment of a COI to investigate human rights violations during and after anti-government demonstrations erupted in February 2011 led to the reinstatement of thousands of dismissed public and private employees and students, the implementation of human rights training for police officers, prosecutors and judges, and the establishment of a special fund for victims.¹⁰¹ While the complete implementation of recommendations is often a long process involving both legal and political mechanisms and a variety of different actors, national fact-finding bodies often create the momentum needed for systematic reforms that individual prosecutions typically do not affect.

---

⁹⁶   *Id.*
⁹⁷   *Id.* ¶ 40.
⁹⁸   This was done in addition to prosecuting the soldiers implicated in the killings. Special Rapporteur on extrajudicial, summary or arbitrary executions, *Civil and Political Rights, Including the Questions of Disappearances and Summary Executions; Rep. of the Special Rapporteur on extrajudicial, summary or arbitrary executions* ¶ 41, U.N. Doc. E/CN.4/2006/53 (Mar. 8, 2006) (by Philip Alston).
⁹⁹   *Id.*
¹⁰⁰ Special Rapporteur on extrajudicial, summary or arbitrary executions, *Question of the violation of human rights and fundamental freedoms in any part of the world, with particular reference to colonial and other dependent countries and territories; Rep. of the Special Rapporteur on extrajudicial, summary or arbitrary executions* ¶ 139, E/CN.4/1993/46 (Dec. 23, 1992) (by Bacre Waly Ndiaye).
¹⁰¹ Bahrain Independent Commission of Inquiry, *Report of the Bahrain Independent Commission of Inquiry* (2011) available at www.bici.org.bh.

Conclusion

The human rights component of the UN system adheres to the values of justice in theory, but in practice it functions as a part of a political process – one in which sometimes adhering to the principles of justice is not in the interests of those driving the institution's machinery. However, as the UN increasingly recognizes the need to promote mechanisms of justice internationally so as to better fulfill its objective of promoting international peace and security and strengthening the respect for human rights, more effective institutions are necessary. Although the mechanisms described above overlap and lack coordination among one another, their potential to collectively strengthen and promote human rights is promising, but only if significant reforms to restructure them are undertaken and best practices are established and implemented uniformly.

Part II:

The Siracusa Guidelines

Guidelines

Objectives and Application of the Siracusa Guidelines

The Siracusa Guidelines seek to promote an effective approach to human rights fact-finding bodies, based on compliance with international best practices. These guidelines are designed to assist in the establishment and operation of fact-finding bodies.

As fact-finding bodies have been and continue to be established by a variety of mechanisms under international, regional and national auspices, all guidelines may not apply to all situations equally. For example the application of certain guidelines may not be required in situations where an existing institutional or administrative framework is already applicable. The mandate of a fact-finding body will also influence the application of the Guidelines, for example, in determining whether applicable law includes human rights law, international humanitarian law, international criminal law or domestic law.

Guideline 1 – Independence and Impartiality

A fact-finding body should maintain its independence and impartiality at all times.

1.1 Independent: A fact-finding body should be free from outside influence.

1.2 Impartial: A fact-finding body should adopt and implement a methodology that allows it to gather facts and draw conclusions in an objective manner.

Guideline 2 – Transparency in Formation

A fact-finding body should be established in a transparent manner that is appropriate to the context for which it is created.

2.1 The following should be made publicly available for the period the fact-finding body is in operation and should be included in the final report:

2.1.1 The organ, body, or agency that established the fact-finding body;

2.1.2 Official establishing instrument (authorizing resolution(s)/ Decree/Law, etc.).

Guideline 3 – Mandate

The fact-finding body should be established by an official document that sets out its mandate and specifies that the fact-finding body is independent and impartial. The mandate should clearly define the objectives, tasks and the expected duration of the fact-finding body. The fact-finding body should be provided with the necessary means and resources to be able to effectively carry out its mandate.

3.1 Wherever possible the mandate should be drafted pursuant to a transparent and consultative process.

3.2 Efforts should be made for all parties involved to consent to the mandate of the fact-finding body.

3.3 The mandate should not prejudge the fact-finding body's work or findings.

3.4 The mandate should clearly define the terms, tasks and objectives of the fact-finding body. The mandate should address the following issues:

3.4.1 The mandate should specify the duration of the fact-finding mission.

3.4.2 The mandate should specify the scope and powers of the investigation. The mandate should afford the fact-finding body the power to access all persons, including public officials, places, records, documents and any other relevant sources of information.

3.4.3 The mandate should require Commissioners to produce a report that should be made public. It should specify whether the report should include recommendations in light of the conclusions of the fact-finding body.

3.4.4 For fact-finding bodies to which the Convention on the Privileges and Immunities of the United Nations of 13 February 1946 does not apply, the mandate should provide all Commissioners and staff of the fact-finding body with such privileges and immunities as are necessary for the fulfillment of their functions, equivalent to those contained in the Convention.

3.5 The mandate should be formulated to enable the fact-finding body to adapt its investigation, consistent with its objectives, to unexpected changes in circumstances, such as changes in applicable law or the emergence of new actors.

3.6 The mandating authority of international fact-finding bodies should call upon relevant State(s) to provide full cooperation with the fact-finding body to facilitate country visits and provide it with access to all individuals and information relevant to the mandate.

3.7 The mandating authority may wish to recommend that a national body take responsibility for implementation of the fact-finding body's recommendations during and after the completion of the mandate by the fact-finding body.

Guideline 4 – Selection of Commissioners

The fact-finding body should be composed in a manner to ensure effective implementation of its mandate. Commissioners should be independent, impartial and possess the qualifications required to carry out the mandate.

4.1 A fact-finding body should be composed of an odd number of Commissioners. The optimal composition of Commissioners should consist of no less than three and no more than five individuals. This is in order to maximize the efficiency of the fact-finding body's work and to allow for majority decision-making in the event that unanimity is not achieved. A leader, or Chair of the Commission, should be selected from the panel at the time all Commissioner appointments are made. The composition of the panel of Commissioners should be diverse, particularly with reference to nationality and gender. Commissioners should preferably be chosen pursuant to a transparent process.

4.2 Commissioners should have the relevant qualifications to carry out their functions effectively. Those may include, individually or collectively, legal, technical and linguistic expertise relevant to the situation, as well as cultural or historical knowledge of the country and experience in dealing with victims of human rights violations.

4.3 The mandating body should make efforts to identify any potential conflicts of interest with respect to the selection of Commissioners. Candidates during the selection process should also disclose any potential conflicts of interest. Any conflict of interest discovered during the selection process that prevents the candidate from acting independently and impartially should preclude the appointment of the candidate.

4.4 Upon selection, each Commissioner should sign a statement affirming that he/she: will carry out his/her functions in an independent, impartial and objective manner; will act in accordance with the mandate; and will take reasonable measures to ensure the highest standards of efficiency, competence and integrity of the mission.

Guideline 5 – Operational Planning

Commissioners should develop an Operational Plan to provide a general roadmap for the operations of the fact-finding body. The Plan should clearly set out the fact-finding body's functions, activities and methods of work.

5.1 Unless already provided, the Operational Plan should set out the employment and accounting policies and procedures that will be established.

5.2 Unless already provided, the Operational Plan should set out the initial budget, which should provide sufficient resources for the fact-finding body to achieve its objectives within the time specified in an efficient and effective manner. If financial resource estimates were undervalued at the time the initial budget was constructed, the fact-finding body should be provided with additional funds.

5.3 The Operational Plan should specify that the fact-finding body will establish and adopt the necessary communication strategies to ensure it meets its objectives.

5.4 The Operational Plan should set out the duties of Commissioners and staff, including the line of communication, to achieve the objectives of the fact-finding body in an efficient and effective manner, and as specified in the mandate.

5.5 The Operational Plan should set out a timeline for the work of the fact-finding body, allocating sufficient time for investigation, deliberation and preparation, and where relevant, translation of the Report and any follow-up that may be required under the mandate.

5.6 The Operational Plan should take account of other internal protocols of the fact-finding body, such as for witness protection, safety and security, employment procedures, the release of evidence and investigation plans, as elaborated under subsequent Guidelines.

5.7 Depending upon the circumstances and needs of the fact-finding body, the Operational Plan may need to be revised or updated during the mission.

Guideline 6 – Recruitment and Management of Staff

The fact-finding body should be provided with the necessary human resources to perform its mandate effectively and within the time allocated to it. All staff should be independent and impartial and should be competent to fulfil the requirements of the position.

6.1 The staff should be selected pursuant to a transparent process with due regard for competence, expertise, experience, diversity, security and familiarity with the language(s) and particular context(s) of the situation. The selection of staff should be made on the basis of the assessed needs of the fact-finding body, particularly with respect to its plan for investigation.

6.2 The staff selected should be available for the time period required to fulfil the tasks assigned to them. In the event it is possible that the mandate may be extended, the fact-finding body should prepare a contingency plan providing for uninterrupted availability of staff to ensure the efficient and effective continuity of the work of the fact-finding body.

6.3 Commissioners should be involved in the selection of senior staff.

6.4 Where the fact-finding body recruits nationals of a State in which the investigation takes place, care should be taken to protect the integrity and independence of the work of the fact-finding body, and the security and privacy of witnesses and other sources of information.

6.5 Where necessary, the fact-finding body should recruit experts in specialized fields, including those with expertise to deal with severely traumatized witnesses who have been victims of crimes, such as sexual violence.

6.6 Where not already provided, and in line with the terms of employment contracts, official complaint, disciplinary and termination procedures should be established.

6.7 All staff should be provided with a written protocol on confidentiality and information security that they should sign prior to commencing their work, upon the extension of employment, or upon changes in the protocol. The protocol should include clear consequences for any breach by the staff. The confidentiality agreement should extend beyond the staff's tenure with the fact-finding body.

6.8 Where not already provided, upon recruitment each staff member should sign a statement disclosing any potential conflicts of interest and affirming that he/she: will carry out his/her functions in an independent, impartial and objective manner; will act in accordance with the mandate, employment contract/terms, and the policies and procedures of the fact-finding body; and will take reasonable measures to ensure the highest standards of efficiency, competence and integrity of the mission.

6.9 Guidelines concerning confidentiality and affirmations of independence, impartiality and objectivity should extend to all external support used by the fact-finding body, including translators and other experts, regardless of whether they were recruited by the fact-finding body.

6.10 Key staff should be briefed before the commencement of the mission to ensure all necessary arrangements are in place, particularly with respect to logistical issues such as transportation, security and communication protocols.

6.11 Before commencing work, staff should be provided, preferably in writing, with information on the policies and procedures of the work of the fact-finding body and, if relevant, with training. This may include policies and training on witness and victim (and relatives of witnesses/victims) protection, the protection and archiving of evidence and other information gathered to ensure their credibility, and techniques for interviewing victims and vulnerable witnesses. Depending upon the circumstances and needs of the fact-finding body, such procedures, policies and training may need to be reinforced, revised or updated during the mission.

6.12 There should be frequent communication between the Commissioners and staff during the work of the fact-finding body. Relevant information should be promptly conveyed by staff to Commissioners. Any decisions relevant to the operations of the fact-finding body should be subject to the approval of the Commissioners.

6.13 Senior staff should periodically review the work of other staff and Commissioners should periodically review the work of senior staff to ensure that proper procedures are being followed and the work is progressing in an efficient manner.

Guideline 7 – Investigation Plan

The fact-finding body should establish an Investigation Plan outlining its strategic objectives, the methodology of the investigation and relevant evidence and other information needed to fulfil the mandate.

7.1 The Investigation Plan should identify allegations of facts or circumstances that should be investigated.

7.2 The Investigation Plan should identify the applicable laws or other obligations that are alleged to have been violated. It should describe the nature of the allegations under investigation and the elements that need to be proven to establish that a violation or crime has occurred.

7.3 The Investigation Plan should identify the priorities of the fact-finding body and the tasks to be completed during the investigation, including methods used to collect evidence and other information.

7.4 The Investigation Plan should identify the resources required to conduct the investigation, including the need for specialized equipment or expertise, such as forensic experts.

7.5 The Investigation Plan should include a protocol for making logistical arrangements needed to carry out the investigation.

7.6 Depending upon the circumstances and needs of the fact-finding body, the Investigation Plan may need to be revised or updated during the mission.

Guideline 8 – Standards for the Collection and Review of Evidence and Other Information

The fact-finding body should adopt standards for the collection, review and evaluation of evidence and other information which provide it with a degree of certainty with regard to its findings. The fact-finding body should also adopt methods for the collection of evidence and other information sufficient to enable an assessment of the reliability of the sources of evidence and other information.

8.1 The fact-finding body should collect evidence and other information that is credible and relevant.

8.2 There should be a protocol for the collection, processing, management, recording and storage of evidence and information, including physical evidence. Physical evidence should be easily identified and located.

8.3 The fact-finding body should establish a protocol regarding the assessment and weighing of evidence and other information. The fact-finding body should clearly articulate the standard it has used to make its findings. The minimum standard for the review and evaluation of evidence and other information should be a balance of probabilities. A balance of probabilities is attained when there is sufficient evidence or other information to reasonably support a finding.

8.4 Evidence or other information that is hearsay evidence, i.e. other than directly from the source, should be distinguished from direct evidence or information. The fact that internal protocols for the fact-finding body may allow consideration of hearsay evidence should not encourage complacency or diminish the importance of locating direct sources of evidence or other information wherever possible.

8.5 Investigators should test and note their own findings regarding the credibility and reliability of witnesses.

8.6 The fact-finding body should establish a chain of custody protocol for physical evidence ensuring that the chain of custody is not broken and that the chronological order of ownership, custody or possession of the physical evidence is recorded.

8.7 Physical evidence should be properly preserved and protected from contamination while in the custody of the fact-finding body.

Guideline 9 – Recording of Evidence and Other Information

The fact-finding body should develop an effective mechanism for the preservation, recording and analysis of evidence and other information, including a database to aid in categorizing and sorting out evidence and other information and their analysis.

9.1 The fact-finding body should develop an effective database system that records evidence and other information obtained from witnesses and through other activities undertaken by the fact-finding body. The database system should be organized to assist with the investigation, provide target/theme-specific information and provide a witness management system to store and track witness statements and information about witnesses.

9.2 Data entry protocols should be established before investigation activities begin and should be designed to ensure that the data will be entered in a standard format. The database system should be easily adaptable to needs as they develop throughout the work of the fact-finding body.

9.3 Where applicable, a witness management system should include, at minimum, the following:
 9.3.1 Brief biographical information.
 9.3.2 Contact details, including a contact person(s) who can reliably contact the witness.
 9.3.3 Protocols to prevent witness record duplication should be implemented, particularly in situations in which a witness may submit multiple statements or when different transliterations of names for the same witness may be used.

9.3.4 Any specific security concerns related to the witness, any reported instances of witness intimidation and information related to witness protection that may have been recorded with regard to any witnesses.

9.3.5 A sequence of events reported by the witness making the statement, in chronological order.

9.3.6 Information on the alleged perpetrator(s).

9.3.7 A comprehensive description of all violations of applicable law or other obligations witnessed, including any words spoken by alleged perpetrator(s) and by other people in the presence of the alleged perpetrator(s).

9.3.8 Information relevant to assisting the fact-finding body in determining the credibility of the witness, including information on the ability and the possibility of the witness to observe/see events or to hear the words the witness is describing in his/her statement.

9.3.9 Physical evidence submitted by the witness should be recorded in accordance with the chain of custody protocol.

9.3.10 Evidence or other information that is hearsay, i.e. other than directly obtained from the source, should be distinguished from direct evidence or testimony.

9.4 A system of evidence numbering should be used to facilitate the recording, access to and management of evidence. The numbering system should be simple and sequential.

Guideline 10 – Witnesses

The fact-finding body should respect the rights of witnesses. It should address and take account of security and potential risks to witnesses by ensuring a safe environment for interview, and taking appropriate measures to guarantee the confidentiality of the identity and the evidence and other information provided to it by witnesses. Special care should be taken with respect to witnesses who have also been victims, particularly victims of sexual violence.

10.1 Witnesses should be informed of the purpose of interview(s).

10.2 Witnesses should be informed that the fact-finding body will produce a Report.

10.3 In taking account of the security and safety of any witness, a preliminary risk assessment should be conducted to determine the level of protection appropriate for the investigation. The witness should be fully informed of the risks and any protection measures available to him/her, and the limitations of those measures. Special care should be taken toward the victims of sexual violence.

10.4 The fact-finding body should approach a witness in a respectful manner that takes into consideration the traumatic nature of the events he/she may have experienced, particularly victims of sexual violence. The fact-finding body should ensure that witnesses who participate in its activities have access to psychological support and advice. In case of particularly vulnerable witnesses, the investigator should receive specialised training in handling such cases. Victims of sexual violence should also be permitted to choose the gender of their interviewer.

10.5 There should be a general presumption in favour of confidentiality of the identity of witnesses, unless the witness has clearly provided his/her informed consent to its disclosure.

10.6 In conducting interviews with witnesses, the following guidelines should apply:

10.6.1 The fact-finding body should take measures to protect the confidentiality and safety of all involved in the interview, including with respect to selecting the location of the interviews.

10.6.2 The fact-finding body should inform each witness of the reasons for the visit or interview, prior to or at the beginning of the meeting, in a language they understand.

10.6.3 Interviews should be scheduled with sufficient time for the ascertainment of all the relevant evidence and other information.

10.6.4 Where possible, interviews should be conducted with at least two Commissioners or staff of the fact-finding body present, not including an interpreter. It should be clarified before the interview whether the witness wishes to have a particular person present, or wishes for a person not to be present during the interview.

10.7 Information obtained during the interview may be recorded in the investigator's notes or be incorporated into a written witness statement. Where a written statement in the first person is obtained, the witness should sign the statement. The witness statement should include an affirmation that he/she has made the statement of his/her own free will, that there has been no threat, promise or inducement that has influenced his/her answers, that he/she has no complaints about his/her treatment during the interview, and that he/she has reviewed the statement and affirms that it is true to the best of his/her knowledge and recollection.

Guidelines

10.8 Where a translator/interpreter was used to translate/interpret a witness statement, the translator/interpreter should sign an affirmation that he/she is a qualified translator/interpreter in the languages that translation/interpretation services have been provided to and from, that the translator/interpreter translated/interpreted the statement, and that the translator/interpreter performed his/her duties to the best of his/her knowledge and abilities.

10.9 Information obtained by Commissioners during meetings with government officials may also need to be treated with confidentiality if the information obtained amounts to state secrets or is of national security concern.

GUIDELINE 11 – INTERNAL REPORTING MANAGEMENT

The fact-finding body should establish protocols for managing internal reporting, including internal periodic reports and special reports that detail the activities of the fact-finding body and call attention to particular issues that require close or immediate attention.

11.1 Periodic reports should be used to provide updates to Commissioners by Senior Staff regarding the fact-finding body's mandate, programs, activities and priorities. Periodic reports should record the activities of the fact-finding body.

11.2 Periodic reports should, at minimum, include the following:
  11.2.1 A summary of each activity conducted by the fact-finding body during the reported period, including, but not limited to, a summary of interviews, statements received, and documents reviewed.
  11.2.2 Where relevant, violations of applicable law and other obligations, including the source(s) of evidence and other information and an assessment of their credibility.
  11.2.3 Meetings conducted, information on the parties present, summary of statements made, if any conclusions drawn, agreements reached, and any follow up action required and/or taken.
  11.2.4 Field visits, including information on the place, incidents observed, evidence or other information collected and statements taken, if any.
  11.2.5 Outreach conducted by the fact-finding body, including statements made by or to the media.

Intersentia

11.2.6 Positive developments that have resulted in the amelioration of the human rights situation the fact-finding body is investigating.
11.2.7 Administrative matters requiring attention.

11.3 Special reports should be used to communicate a specific issue that requires immediate action or closer attention.
11.4 Special reports should include, at minimum, the following:
11.4.1 Source(s) of evidence or other information and an assessment of reliability.
11.4.2 Identification of the violations of applicable law or other obligations that are implicated and may require urgent attention.
11.4.3 Analysis of the situation, including if the situation or the event falls within a pattern, if relevant.
11.4.4 Conclusions and recommendations for further action, if any.

Guideline 12 – Safety

The safety and security of witnesses, Commissioners and staff of the fact-finding body, as well as of the evidence and other information collected, should be considered at all times.

12.1 Where necessary and feasible, a reconnaissance team should be deployed to conduct an assessment of the general risk faced by witnesses, Commissioners and staff of the fact-finding body prior to the commencement of activities.
12.2 A safety plan should be developed prior to the commencement of the work of the fact-finding body. Where possible, this safety plan should be developed with the support of and in collaboration with the mandating body and other relevant bodies/agencies that may provide assistance. The safety plan should be regularly updated.
12.3 A protocol should be developed to protect the identity and physical safety of witnesses. The protocol should address any measures that will need to be taken by the mandating body or another authority to maintain the safety of witnesses after the fact-finding body has concluded its work.
12.4 Commissioners and staff of the fact-finding body should be made aware of the potential risks during the mission and should be notified of the safety plan for emergencies prior to the commencement of their duties.
12.5 Commissioners and staff of the fact-finding body should be provided with security briefings periodically throughout the mission.

12.6 Commissioners and staff of the fact-finding body should receive training on responding to emergency situations.
12.7 The fact-finding body should provide its Commissioners and staff with the necessary equipment to maintain their safety in the field.
12.8 Commissioners and staff of the fact-finding body should be provided with adequate insurance coverage that applies to all risks faced, particularly where the mission is conducted in a potentially dangerous area.

Guideline 13 – Reporting

The Report should present the purpose, formation, operations and method of work of the fact-finding body, as well as evidence and other information compiled during the investigation. While protecting the confidentiality and anonymity of sources, it should contain a detailed record of events and their analysis. The Report should also set out findings on whether violations of applicable law or other obligations have occurred, and may make conclusions in light of its findings. If relevant to the mandate, it should recommend measures to be taken. Where required by the mandate, interim or periodic reports may also be submitted by the fact-finding body.

Information Required
13.1 The Report should include information on the formation of the fact-finding body, such as: its mandate and Operational Plan; the process of the selection of Commissioners and staff, including affirmations of the independence and impartiality of Commissioners pursuant to Guideline 4.4.
13.2 The Report should indicate how evidence and other information will be secured after the conclusion of the work of the fact-finding body, and how confidentiality will be preserved (for example by placing the archives for safe-keeping with a third party institution).
13.3 The Report should include a description of the organization and method of work of the fact-finding body, including the investigation methodology and activities, as well as the initial and final budget of the fact-finding body.
13.4 The Report should include a description of any facilitating or hindering factors the fact-finding body encountered in the course of its work, including those that affected the efficiency of its work and the reliability of its findings, such as:

13.4.1 Refusal of an implicated state to cooperate with the fact-finding body and the implications.
13.4.2 Cooperation of or interference by central or local government, foreign governments, armed tribes, the international organizations, local institutions, NGOs or any other party.
13.4.3 Factors that may have affected the credibility of information, particularly witness intimidation and conducting interviews on 'non-neutral ground'.
13.4.4 Lack of access (whether to sites, people, documents, etc.) and the reason for it.
13.4.5 Any other concurrent missions to the state in question or neighbouring states and the fact-finding body's cooperation, if any, with such missions.

13.5 The Report may include a description of relevant historical, social, political and economic contexts of the area covered by its mandate to provide a better understanding of the content of its Report. The Report should cite the sources from which such information is obtained and provide an analysis of the reliability of those sources.

Findings

13.6 Findings should be grounded in facts and applicable law or other obligations. Where appropriate, findings may include:
13.6.1 An objective statement of all the relevant facts discovered by the Commission, references to the sources of those facts, including an analysis of the reliability of those sources (for example, if the information was hearsay, drawn from secondary sources, doubts regarding the credibility of witnesses, etc.) and how the facts were verified and cross-checked before they were relied upon (for example, if corroborating information was obtained, etc.).
13.6.2 Situations where there are conflicting facts or where the evidence or other information was inconclusive.
13.6.3 A clear statement of the applicable law or other obligations relied upon, and where appropriate, the elements required to establish the violation or crime, a reference to the sources of that law, and sufficient detail regarding the facts to enable the reader to understand the conclusions reached by the fact-finding body.
13.6.4 A critical assessment, where appropriate, of the capacity of institutional structures, policies and practices, including of the national justice system, to investigate and prosecute the violations found by the fact-finding body, if any.

Recommendations

13.7 Where required by the mandate, the Report should make recommendations that promote transparency and accountability, prevent future human rights violations, take into account of the rights and needs of victims, foster respect for the rule of law and human rights, and encourage national reconciliation.

    13.7.1 The Report should note any steps that have already been taken by officials or non-state actors that contribute to the implementation of the recommendations.

    13.7.2 Recommendations should focus on concrete and specific actions to address the findings. The Report should explain the reasons for each recommendation, drawing upon the facts, analysis and conclusions of the Report.

    13.7.3 Where required by the mandate, the Report should recommend an action plan for the follow-up on the recommendations, including a timeline that would ensure that follow-up is initiated as soon as practicable after submission of the Report.

    13.7.4 The Report should recommend measures, including mechanisms, to be put in place to ensure protection and support are offered on an on-going basis to victims, witnesses and staff.

13.8 The Report may indicate whether the conclusions and recommendations are unanimous.

Publication and Dissemination

13.9 The report, along with any recommendations, should be published, translated if necessary, and widely disseminated.

13.10 The fact-finding body should consider providing a summary of the report along with the report itself, if the report is lengthy. Where the mandate imposes a page limitation for the Report, the fact-finding body should consider the use of annexes and attachments to supplement information.

GUIDELINE 14 – ARCHIVES

All notes, transcripts and documents, including electronic evidence and other information, together with other materials from the work of the fact-finding body, should be kept secure at all times. The fact-finding body should make arrangements to ensure that such evidence and other information remain secure after the conclusion of its work.

Part III:

An Empirical Analysis of United Nations Commissions of Inquiry: Toward the Development of a Standardized Methodology

An Empirical Analysis of United Nations Commissions of Inquiry: Toward the Development of a Standardized Methodology[1]

Prepared by Michelle Martin[2] & Leticia Villarreal Sosa[3]

Abstract

This study evaluates the UN's approach to rule of law, specifically, its mechanisms for investigating alleged human rights abuses through international Commissions of Inquiry. The present study involved the evaluation and in-depth comparative analysis of 31 Commissions of Inquiry, which included 30 UN Commissions of Inquiry and one national commission of inquiry, investigating past allegations of human rights abuses. The Commissions of Inquiry reports were subjected to a comparative analysis using a multi-methods approach. While the results revealed some methodological strengths, numerous methodological deficits were noted, reflecting both inconsistencies in how investigations are implemented and facilitated, as well as in the reporting of findings. Recommendations are made regarding ways in which noted challenges of investigating alleged human rights abuses on an international and national level can be addressed in order to strengthen best practices in human rights fact-finding missions and report compilation.

---

[1] The authors wish to thank Dominican University students Maxine Davis, Francis Arthur Amy Voege, Taryn Batherson, Lubna Saleh, and Jessica Butler for their work as research assistants, their helpful suggestions and advice in earlier drafts of this manuscript.
[2] Ph.D. (cand), M.S.W., M.Soc.Sci.
[3] Ph.D., L.C.S.W.

Introduction

This study evaluates the UN's approach to rule of law, specifically, its mechanisms for investigating alleged human rights abuses on an international level. The area of international human rights has received significant attention in recent decades, with particular focus on the response of the international community to mass human rights violations, including crimes against humanity. The reasons for this increased attention is rooted in a range of global dynamics, chief among them a sharp increase in armed civil conflict, particularly in the Global South. In fact, in the past three decades there have been between 16 and 33 armed conflicts at any one time, predominantly in the Global South.[4] This new pattern of violence reflects a significant departure from traditional Cold War inter-state conflict over territory, and toward a new type of conflict that often is ethnonationalist in nature, and extends well beyond borders.[5]

Ethnonationalist conflict is qualitatively different than traditional inter-state conflict, frequently with more severe consequences. Research clearly indicates that conflicts involving identity, beliefs, values and cultural norms often results in conflicts that are more violent and protracted, and less likely to be resolved through traditional conflict resolution strategies. As such, ethnonationalist conflict tends to be far more violent, frequently involving mass human rights violations, often rising to the level of crimes against humanity,[6] ranging from political persecution, massacres of entire villages and ethnic cleanings, to genocide.[7] Many women and girls are raped as a tactic of war,[8] children are conscripted into armed conflict,[9] men are often targeted as threats and killed, and elders and the physically weak often

---

[4] Stockholm International Peace Research Institute (SIPRI), Yearbook of World Armaments.
[5] Danielle Conservi, "Ethnonationalism in the Contemporary World," Routledge Advances in International Relations and Global Politics. (2007): 288. Taylor & Francis. Kindle Edition.
[6] See M. Cherif Bassiouni, "Crimes Against Humanity: The Case for a Specialized Convention," 9 WASH. U. GLOB. STUD. L. REV. 575 (2010), http://digitalcommons.law.wustl.edu/globalstudies/vol9/iss4/2 for a more in-depth discussion of the increase in mass violence in response to conflict.
[7] Alex Bellamy, "Mass Atrocities and Armed Conflict: Links, Distinctions, and Implications for the Responsibility to Prevent", *The Stanley Foundation*, (2011), available online at: http://www.stanleyfoundation.org/publications/pab/BellamyPAB22011.pdf.
[8] Colleen Kivlahan K. and Nate Ewigman, "Rape as a weapon of war in modern conflicts," *BMJ*, (2010): 340:c3270.
[9] Theresa Stichick Betancourt, Ivelina Ivanova Borisova, Timothy Philip Williams, Robert Brennan, Theodore Whitfield, Marie De La Soudiere, John Williamson, Stephen Gilman. "Sierra Leone's Former Child Soldiers: A Follow-Up Study of Psychosocial Adjustment and Community Reintegration". *Child Dev*, 81 (2010): 1077–1095.

perish due to harsh circumstances.[10] Additionally, millions are victims of forced displacement. In fact, in 2010 the United Nations High Commission for Refugees (UNCHR) estimated that there were approximately 43.7 million individuals who were forcibly displaced from their homes across international borders, representing an increase over prior years.[11] The recent surge in international conflict, and the violence associated with new patterns of conflict, warrants increased attention from the international community, particularly with regard to the development of investigative methods that conform to best practice principles, and reduce the chance of renewed conflict and human rights abuse, while holding perpetrators of human rights violations accountable.

Historic responses to situations involving mass human rights violations were largely unstructured and often unsuccessful until the implementation of the UN Charter in 1945, and the subsequent adoption of the UDHR in 1948.[12] Since the adoption of the UDHR, the UN has increasingly conceptualized the respect for, and promotion of rule of law on national and international levels as the heart of its mission within its three pillars – peace and security, development, and human rights.[13] The UN's rule of law work is vast and complex, and includes such activities as assisting Member States with the development and strengthening of its social institutions,[14] monitoring member States' implementation and adherence to human rights treaty bodies and optional protocols,[15] and engagement in the monitoring and investigation of alleged human rights abuses with the goal of holding

---

[10] Steven Fox and Sharon Tang. "The Sierra Leonean refugee experience: traumatic events and psychiatric sequelae. Journal of Nervous and Mental Disease", 188, (2000): 490–495; Nicholas Sambanis, Marta Reynal-Querol, Håvard Hegre, Lani Elliott, Paul Collier and Anke Hoeffler. "Breaking the Conflict Trap: Civil War and Development Policy," New Policy Research Report (2003).

[11] UN High Commissioner for Refugees, (UNHCR) Global Trends 2010, (June 2011), accessed 1 September 2011 http://www.unhcr.org/refworld/docid/4e01b00e2.html.

[12] *See* Program on Humanitarian Policy and Conflict Research (HPCR), Harvard University, "HPCR Working Paper: Building Effective Monitoring, Reporting, and Face-finding Mechanisms" *SSRN* (2012), accessed January 1, 2013, http://ssrn.com/abstract=2038854 for a discussion of formalized fact-finding missions initiated in 1913 by the Carnegie Endowment International Peace to investigate the Balkan Wars of 1912 and 1913, and the 1931 League of Nations Lytton Commission investigating the conflict between China and Japan.

[13] "United Nations Rule of Law website, http://www.un.org/en/ruleoflaw/index.shtml (accessed December 10, 2012).

[14] Department of Peacekeeping Operations and Office of High Commissioner for Human Rights. *United Nations Rule of Law Indicators: Implementation Guide and Project Tools.* United Nations Publishing, 2011, http://www.un.org/en/peacekeeping/publications/un_rule_of_law_indicators.pdf (accessed December 21, 2012).

[15] UN Monitoring the Core International Human Rights Treaties, http://www.ohchr.org/EN/HRBodies/Pages/TreatyBodies.aspx (accessed 21 December, 2012).

perpetrators accountable through various judicial mechanisms. Further, the UN is increasingly engaged on a national level providing operational, monitoring and investigative support within the context of "peacemaking, peacekeeping post-crisis, and peacebuilding to long-term development."[16]

UN Monitoring, Reporting and Fact-finding Activities

The engagement in rule of law mechanisms is rather unwieldy and compartmentalized, with over 40 different UN entities coordinated by 10 UN agencies that engage in rule of law work.[17] As of October 2012 the UN was providing rule of law assistance to more than 150 Member States, within a variety of contexts, including "development, conflict, post-conflict and peacebuilding situations, including 17 peace operations with rule-of-law mandates."[18] Examples include the UN providing assistance to Somalia in its constitution-making processes,[19] as well as peacekeeping missions in the Democratic Republic of Congo, and Darfur.[20] Further, the UN engages in MRF activities within a variety of contexts. For instance, peacekeeping missions often engage in monitoring and reporting activities, within the context of alleged or potential violations of international law, or while mapping past violations.[21]

The UN also engages in fact-finding missions, primarily to investigate past alleged human rights abuses. UN fact-finding missions have been

---

[16] Report of the Secretary-General, *Strengthening and Coordinating United Nations Rule of Law Activities*, (2008):14, accessed January 1, 2013 http://daccess-dds-ny.un.org/doc/UNDOC/GEN/N08/452/71/PDF/N0845271.pdf?OpenElement.
[17] According to the United Nations, all rule of law work falls under falls under the auspices of the 'Rule of Law Coordination and Resource Group', chaired by the Deputy Secretary-General. The Group consists of 10 different UN agencies, including the Department of Political Affairs (DPA), the Department of Peacekeeping Operations (DPKO), Office of the High Commissioner for Human Rights (OHCHR), the Office of Legal Affairs (OLA), United Nations Development Programme (UNDP), The United Nations Children's Fund (UNICEF), The Office of the United Nations High Commissioner for Refugees (UNHCR), the United Nations Development Fund for Women (UNIFEM) and the United Nations Office on Drugs and Crime (UNODC) (see UN Rule of Law website at: http://www.un.org/en/ruleoflaw/index.shtml).
[18] "Deputy Secretary-General, Addressing Sixth Committee, says United Nations Has Comparative Advantage in Providing Rule-Of-Law Assistance to Member States," United Nations press release, October 11, 2012, on the United Nations website, http://www.un.org/News/Press/docs/2012/dsgsm645.doc.htm.
[19] Ibid.
[20] *See* Security Council Resolution 1925 (MONUCSO), and 1769 (UNAMID), respectively.
[21] MONUSCO's 2010 'Mapping Exercise', and more recent reports on alleged arms violations in the DRC are examples.

defined as "any activity designed to obtain detailed knowledge of the relevant facts of any dispute or situation which the competent UN organs need in order to exercise effectively their functions in relation to the maintenance of international peace and security."[22] The integrity of any fact-finding mission's investigation into alleged violations of human rights is wholly dependent upon the principles of neutrality, impartiality, and independence, where fact-finding bodies "independently, objectively and impartially collect relevant information, confirm its veracity, and analyze this information to produce credible evidence about violations, their causes and effects, as well as identify their perpetrators."[23] The goal of any fact-finding mission is the production of a report that provides an "objective and complete representation of the circumstances surrounding a given act."[24]

The UN commonly commissions fact-finding missions as international commissions of inquiry – ad hoc non-judicial fact-finding bodies implemented in relation to a conflict in order to investigate relevant events and possible violations of international law. Commissions of inquiry may also be commissioned at national and regional levels. In fact, national commissions of inquiry are considered an important first step in the investigation of allegations of human rights abuses, and are considered a powerful tool in not only addressing human rights situations, but also resolving conflict, if the investigations are handled appropriately.[25]

Although UN MRF activities can be facilitated through various UN bodies, the primary bodies through which the UN promotes and manages international human rights compliance are the OHCHR and the HRC.[26] UN Member States created the OHCHR in 1993 through General Assembly resolution A/RES/48/141. The OHCHR is a part of the Secretariat structure of the UN and reports to the UNSC. The OHCHR mandates MRF missions

---

[22] See the Declaration on fact-finding by the United Nations in the *Field of the Maintenance of International Peace and Security*, adopted in 1991, 66.
[23] UNHCHR, "Human Rights Investigations and their Methodology: Lecture by Ms. Navanethem Pillay United Nations High Commissioner for Human Rights", UNISPAL Document Collection (February 24, 2010) accessed January 2, 2013 http://unispal.un.org/UNISPAL.NSF/0/C9222F058467E6F6852576D500574710.
[24] Théo Boutruche, "Credible Fact-Finding and Allegations of International Humanitarian Law Violations: Challenges in Theory and Practice", *Journal of Conflict & Security Law* 16, no. 1 (2011): 105–140.
[25] Geneva Academy of International Humanitarian Law, "The UN Human Rights Council: Commissions of Inquiry Conference brief" (presentation, Human Rights Day Conference The UN Human Rights Council: Commissions of Inquiry Dec. 1, 2011) accessed January 4, 2013 http://www.geneva-academy.ch/docs/news/HR-council-inquiry-conference-brief.pdf.
[26] The Commission for Human Rights was replaced by the Human Rights Commission on April 3, 2006 by General Assembly Resolution A/RES/60/251.

and provides support for other UN mandating agencies. The HRC was created in 2006 by the UNGA as an inter-governmental body that focuses on cooperation and dialogue to assist "member states meet their human rights obligations through dialogue, capacity building, and technical assistance."[27] It also makes recommendations on the development of international human rights laws. The HRC is comprised of Member States that are elected to serve on the Council by the UNGA. Currently there are 47 council seats representing various geographical regions. The HRC addresses specific country concerns through Special Procedures mandates pertaining to specific countries and situations, which are then managed and facilitated by OHCHR Special Rapporteurs.[28] Currently there are 36 thematic mandates[29] and 12 country mandates.[30] While the OHCHR may take the lead in many fact-finding investigations into specific country situations involving alleged human rights abuses, the OHCHR's mandate renders it responsible for taking "the lead to rationalize, adapt, strengthen and streamline the UN human rights machinery."[31]

In order to analyze the effectiveness of international fact-finding missions, it is important to first understand the range of MRF activities most often engaged in on a national and international level, in response to human rights situations. Harvard University's Program on Humanitarian Policy and Conflict Research (HPCR) has developed a conceptual framework to better understand the role and function of MRF activities in response to what they cite as the often difficult process of distinguishing between various types of international MRF missions, which will have significantly different mandates with regard to their respective "strategic goals, the standard of evidence required, and the nature of their mission's relationship with its investigative targets,"[32] depending upon their mandated parameters and objectives.

The conceptual framework categorizes MRF activities based on a goal structure, as well as the strategies used to facilitate each type of activity's

---

[27] "FAQs on the Human Rights Council," UN News Centre, accessed January 3, 2013, http://www.un.org/News/dh/infocus/hr_council/hr_q_and_a.htm.
[28] See "Special Procedures of the Human Rights Council," http://www.ohchr.org/EN/HRBodies/SP/Pages/Welcomepage.aspx.
[29] See UN 'Special Procedure' Thematic Mandates, http://www.ohchr.org/EN/HRBodies/SP/Pages/Themes.aspx.
[30] See UN 'Special Procedure' Country Mandates, http://www.ohchr.org/EN/HRBodies/SP/Pages/Countries.aspx.
[31] OHCHR Management Plan 2012–2013. OHCHR, 9, accessed January 4, 2013 http://www2.ohchr.org/english/ohchrreport2011/web_version/media/pdf/2_About_OHCHR.pdf.
[32] HPCR Working Paper, 10.

mandate. For instance, *monitoring* activities, which are most commonly associated with UN peacekeeping missions, focus on *prevention*, and rely on prevention strategies, while providing *supportive dialogue* to target parties. Human rights monitors seek information, looking for *patterns* that might indicate that human rights abuses have occurred, or are about to occur. If the potential for human rights abuses is noted, they engage in supportive dialogue with target parties with the goal of prevention. By comparison, *reporting* activities *mitigate* situations of ongoing human rights violations. While human rights monitors serve in the capacity of *advisor* to the target parties, human rights actors involved in reporting activities examine facts within the context of specific allegations of human rights abuses, such as the case of Special Procedures, but may be a part of peace-keeping missions as well as an extension of the monitoring process. The goal of reporting activities is to diminish the risk of future violations by advising target parties on ways that future human rights abuses can be avoided, by "convince[ing] alleged perpetrators to alter their behavior".[33]

Finally, *fact-finding* activities utilize *corrective strategies*, by engaging in comprehensive investigations in response to UN resolutions (or mandates by national governments), with the goal of making alleged perpetrators *accountable* for their crimes. Fact-finding missions are primarily facilitated by a UN agency or body within the framework of a formal mandate, which stipulates the parameters of the mission. Fact-finding is a more narrow activity than monitoring, entailing "a great deal of information gathering in order to establish and verify the facts surrounding an alleged human rights violation," where the reliability of the findings depends on "accepted procedures" by establishing a reputation for fairness and impartiality.[34] According to the HRC, the primary objectives of fact-finding commissions of inquiries are to:

1. Establish impartially whether violations of human rights law and/or humanitarian law have occurred;
2. Investigate whether or not violations are systematic and widespread;
3. Report on a State's ability to deal with the violations;
4. Highlight the root causes of the situation;
5. Suggest ways of moving forward; and
6. Produce a historical record of events that have occurred.[35]

---

[33] HPCR Working Paper, 12.
[34] See OHCHR, "Professional Training Manual No. 7: Training Manual on Human Rights Monitoring. United Nations, Geneva", 2001: 9.
[35] Geneva Academy of International Humanitarian Law, "The UN Human Rights Council".

The international community, particularly the UN, has increasingly relied upon fact-finding missions, most notably COIs in order to investigate situations of potential mass human rights violations, particularly crimes against humanity. Despite this pattern of increasing reliance, numerous scholars have cited serious concerns about the ways in which such missions are implemented and facilitated.[36] Bassiouni notes how the UN approach to fact-finding can be problematic, noting that the political nature of the UN often results in its activities being driven by the political interests of Member Countries, particularly those in the West.[37] Bassiouni points out that while UN human rights mechanisms are rooted in the values of truth and justice, these values can be easily compromised through "political oversight,"[38] which is inherent in the fact-finding process. Bassiouni notes that far too often missions and mandates are constructed in ways that are "politically convenient...[and]... give only the appearance of pursuing these values while at the same time not generating politically unwanted results".[39] In this sense, the protection and enforcement of international human rights becomes just one more tool of *realpolitik*.[40] In fact, Baily notes that far too often in regard to UN investigations "facts are being sought not to allay ignorance, but to provide fresh ammunition in a political struggle"[41]

Challenges in the implementation and facilitation of fact-finding missions, including ineffective management, and internal and external pressures and influences, can result in a damaged and compromised investigative process, which has serious ramifications on the justice process. Challenges that are not appropriately addressed create risks to neutrality and impartiality, as well as negatively affecting witnesses and victims. Developing effective ways of managing common challenges experienced in fact-finding missions contributes to what Bassiouni points out as "one of the most important and yet overlooked goals of [international criminal justice]", which is "to bring closure to victims and provide them with redress".[42]

The lack of empirical research into how MRF missions and activities, particularly fact-finding missions, are implemented and facilitated, including how various internal and external influences determine outcomes, renders

---

[36] Rob Grace and Claude Bruderlein, "On Monitoring, Reporting and Fact-finding Mechanisms", *ESIL Reflections*, 1 no. 2 (2012): 2–5.
[37] Bassiouni, "Appraising UN-justice".
[38] Ibid., 36.
[39] Ibid.
[40] Lei Guang, "Realpolitik Nationalism International Sources of Chinese Nationalism" *Modern China*, 31, no. 4 (2005): 487–514.
[41] Bailey, "UN Fact-finding", 250.
[42] M. Cherif Bassiouni, "Perspectives on International Criminal Justice", 50 VA. *J. INT'L L.* 269 (2010).

any reliable analysis of OHCHR and HRC approaches to international human rights investigations difficult, yet several international human rights scholars agree that such analyses are vitally important in order to provide insights and guidance to the international human rights community. Such insights and guidance can then contribute to the further development of investigative mechanisms and procedures.[43] The present study is an attempt to contribute to the growing body of literature that examines and analyzes the UN approach to international human rights investigations, with the goal of further developing best practice methodology.

Methods

The present study involved the evaluation and in-depth comparative analysis of 31 COIs, including 30 UN COIs and one national COI, investigating past allegations of human rights abuses. The decision to conduct a comparative evaluation of COIs rather than examining different types of MRF activities, was based upon various factors, including the conclusion that an analysis of one type of fact-finding mission with similar objectives is the best foundational approach to analyzing the UN's approach to rule of law and fact-finding, with subsequent studies potentially focusing on inter-MRF activity comparisons.

UN international COIs were selected from the pool of reports available on UN websites, within the public domain. The national COI was selected due to its comprehensive nature (see Appendix 1 for a complete list of COIs included in the study).[44] The data evaluated in the sample was subjected to content analysis in order to explore comparative trends and patterns between the selected investigations. The content analysis yielded a total of 40 variables that were deemed key to the facilitation of the fact-finding investigations. The study analyzed both the nature of the investigation as well as the construction of the COI reports, with regard to their overall structure and comprehensive nature (see Appendix 2 for a comprehensive list of variables analyzed in question format). Once key variables were identified they were operationalized to reflect best practice as reflected in the literature, as well as in a way that was practical based upon the data (see Appendix 3 for the operationalization of the variables).

---

[43] Bassiouni, "Appraising UN-justice"; Robertson, "Human Rights and Fact Finding"; HPCR Working Paper.
[44] A pilot study was conducted on 22 COI reports prior to the present study, which yielded important information on methodological challenges. The pilot study informed the current methodology used in this study.

Intersentia

Variables related to the following aspects of the investigation or report compilation, and included the following: investigation duration, number of pages in the report, whether a summary of facts was included in the report, whether a list of human rights violations alleged to have been committed was included in the report, whether submission of the evidence was documented, whether facts were established and conclusions reached, whether the subject State(s) consented to the investigation, and whether the subject State and the UN enter into an agreed terms of engagement, whether there was a prior or simultaneous investigation into the same incident(s), whether there were any follow-up investigation mandates, and whether the report provided explicit information on the methodology used in the investigation. Variables relating to mission personnel included whether total numbers of personnel, names, and background information were included in the report, as well as whether codes of conduct and conflict of interest checks were performed (and whether this information was included in the final reports). Variables relating to witnesses and victims included whether the investigative team had access to all witnesses and victims, and detainees, as well as all relevant physical sites, whether witnesses and victims were vetted, whether they were provided with privacy (confidentiality) and protection, and whether this information was sufficiently documented in the COI report. Finally, variables related to financial resources and budget management were included, such as whether the budget was included in the report, or was available within the public domain, and whether the budgets were audited and by whom.

Each report was analyzed by two different reviewers, with each variable being coded reflecting a response of "yes", "no", or "not included in the report". If the two reviewers coded a variable differently, the report was subjected to a third review. If a conflict could not be resolved (most often due to a lack of clarity in the report), the research team met and discussed the nature of the conflict and a collective decision was made. Further, a reference to the cause of the conflict was then noted in the qualitative review for further analysis.

Data was collected on an Excel sheet posted in Google Docs, which reduced the possibility for data entry error (elevated due to the length of some reports, the number of variables being rated, and the denseness of the Excel data entry logs). STATA was used for the descriptive statistics yielding frequency distributions and measures of central tendency of each variable, which allowed for comparisons along a continuum of variables, so that patterns of investigative practices and report compilation could be observed and analyzed.

The qualitative analysis of the data occurred primarily in two ways. Irregularities and inconsistencies contained in the reports were noted upon quantitative review. Thus when the quantitative analysis yielded conflicting results, the research team noted issues that resulted in lacking clarity in the evaluation of the 40 variables for the purposes of evaluating subjectivity surrounding the quantitative variables. The other approach to qualitative analysis involved each reviewer noting themes and patterns in both the investigation activities, and the compilation of the report. Such themes related to the nature and construction of the mandate, personnel hiring practices, standardization of methodology (including inconsistencies), management of evidence, the management of witnesses, victims and detainees, the role of NGOs in the investigation, the structure and compilation of the report, and the nature of recommendations and follow-up practices (see Appendix 4).

Results

Mandates

Report reviewers noted that most of the mandates were unclear and ambiguous, with language that was often too general to provide sufficient guidance to fact-finding commissioners. Further, the ambiguity of the mandates appeared to render the development of measurable objectives challenging. For example, the Commission established to investigate post-election violence in Kenya[45] ("Kenya Commission") was mandated to (i) investigate the facts and circumstances surrounding the violence between 28 December 2007 and 28 February 2008, (ii) investigate the conduct of State security agencies in their handling of it and (iii) to recommend measures with regard to bringing to justice those persons responsible for criminal acts. The mandate appears quite general, lacking parameters regarding the violence to be investigated, which could have informed the fact-finding commission by providing boundaries in terms of the breadth of their investigative activities. For instance, was the mandate instructing the commissioners to investigate all violence even remotely associated with the elections, or violence within a particular context (i.e., political)? The ambiguous nature of the mandate may render any analysis of whether the Kenya Commission extended beyond the boundaries of the mandate quite challenging. Complicating this issue even further is the fact that the Kenya Commission report, "Report from OHCHR Fact-Finding Mission to Kenya,

---

[45] Report from OHCHR Fact-Finding mission to Kenya, 6–28 February 2008.

6–28 February 2008" included only the first component of the mandate ("to investigate the facts and circumstances surrounding the violence between 28 December 2007 and 28 February 2008"), omitting the latter two components of the mandate, rendering it even more challenging to effectively evaluate the Kenya Commission's interpretation of the mandate, and whether the Commission remained within the intended scope of the mandate.

This example reflects several problematic issues in regard to the construction of fact-finding mission mandates in addition to ambiguous language, including how mandates were negotiated, and developed, as well as what criteria were used to determine their scope. Additionally, references in the report regarding how commissioners interpreted the mandates is vital to being able to assess the Commission's effectiveness in fulfilling a fact-finding missions' mandate, and this information was often absent in the COI reports analyzed. Consistent with the Kenya Commission report, in many reports, the mandate was frequently omitted, or was only included in part. While including a good paraphrase of the mandate may offer the advantage of being more concise and readable, if an exact quotation of the mandate is not included the reader is unable to effectively evaluate the actual mandate contained in the UN resolution as a comparison. Further, a poor paraphrase may contribute to an impression of lacking transparency, rendering it a challenge to evaluate whether the commissioners faithfully interpreted the precise language of the mandate contained in the UN resolution.

For instance, the "Report of the high-level fact-finding mission to Beit Hanoun established under Council resolution S-3/1" ("Beit Hanoun Commission") included a paraphrase of the mandate with an extensive discussion focusing on how the Beit Hanoun Commission's interpretation of the mandate, but failed to include a quotation of the actual mandate contained in the UN resolution, making it difficult to evaluate the Commissioners' interpretation. By contrast, the "Report of the International Fact-Finding Mission to Investigate Violations of International Law, Including International Humanitarian and Human Rights Law, Resulting from the Israeli Attacks on the Flotilla of Ships Carrying Humanitarian Assistance" ("Flotilla Commission") included a direct quotation of the mandate from the relevant UN resolution as well as a discussion regarding concerns of the Flotilla Commission regarding potential bias contained in the mandate. The report included a comprehensive rationale for the mandate interpretation, which appeared thoughtful and articulate, because it provided greater context and understanding of the Commissioners' ultimate interpretation of the mandate. The "Bahrain Independent Commission of Inquiry" ("Bahrain Commission") is an additional example of a COI with a clearly articulated mandate, that was easy to read, and included manageable objectives, all of which was comprehensively included in the final COI report.

State Consent

Thirty of the reports evaluated (96.9%) included information about whether the State involved in the investigation consented to the investigation. Of these 30 reports, seven (22.5%) reported that the subject State did not consent to the investigation while 22 of the reports (71%) stated that the subject State did consent to the investigation. Just over half of the reports (16/51.6%) included no reference to the existence of a 'Terms of Engagement' agreement between the subject State and the fact-finding mission, with only seven reports (22.5%) referencing that a 'Terms of Engagement' agreement existed, and eight (25.8%) stating that 'Terms of Engagement' agreement did not exist.

State consent, and its subsequent cooperation contributed to the success of the mission in a variety of ways, most significantly in whether the investigative team was permitted into the country, but also with regard to whether the team was granted access to physical sites relevant to the investigation, as well as being granted open access to witnesses, victims and detainees. In general, the majority of the reports noted whether or not a subject State had consented to the investigation, but few reports included any reference to whether any terms of engagement were negotiated, and if so, what the nature of those terms were. Thus, in most reports it remained unclear just how cooperative the subject State was of the mission, and whether there were any overt or covert pressures placed upon the investigative team (as well as witnesses and victims), and whether such pressures or influence may have impeded the investigation. An exception to this pattern was the "Study of Reported Violations of Human Rights in Chile, with Particular Reference to Torture and other Cruel, Inhuman or Degrading Treatment or Punishment", where the Chilean government's resistance to the fact-finding mission was clearly articulated in the report, as was the impact of their lacking cooperation on the nature of the investigation.

Prior and Simultaneous Investigations

Eighteen of the reports (58%) made no reference to whether a prior human rights inquiry had been conducted in the region regarding the same incident, whereas 10 of the reports (32.2%) did reference the existence of a prior inquiry, and three of the reports (9.7%) stipulated hat there were no prior inquiries. Most of the reports that did reference a prior investigation did not make clear whether that inquiry was on a national level. Twenty-three of the reports (74.1%) did not include any information about whether simultaneous investigations were occurring in the subject State or region. Among the eight reports that did include this information, four of the reports (12.9%) indicated that there had been a simultaneous investigation while four reports (12.9%) indicated there had not been a simultaneous investigation. Nineteen reports (61.3%) did not make any reference to follow-up monitoring or investigation. Ten reports (32.2%) stated that a follow-up investigation was mandated, while two reports (6.5%) stated that a mandated follow-up was not required.

The majority of the reports included either no information or included only vague references to the existence of other national or international investigations focusing on the same or related incidences of alleged human rights abuses. For instance, the "Report of the United Nations High Commissioner for Human Rights on the Situation of Human Rights in Côte d'Ivoire" ("Côte d'Ivoire Commission") included a vague reference to other UN organizations and NGOs working in the country simultaneous to the COI mission, but it was unclear whether these organizations were conducting simultaneous investigations of the same incidents of alleged human rights abuses, or whether the purpose of their work was unrelated to the work of the Côte d'Ivoire Commission.

Terms of Reference

A Terms of Reference stipulates a fact-finding mission's activities and methods, including how a particular investigation will be carried out, and by whom. One of the most foundational components of a mission's Terms of Reference is the length of the mission and the timeline of the mission. Among the reports evaluated, 12 of the reports (38.7%) did not include any clear information about the duration of the investigation, thus it was difficult to discern the start date and end date of these fact-finding missions. Of the 20 reports (64.5%) that did include information about the duration of the mission, the mean length was 138 days, the shortest duration was nine days, and the longest duration was 526 days, with a standard deviation of 122 days, illustrating the wide range in duration of the missions.

Even when reports included specific date parameters, it was unclear as to what event lay within the period of investigation, and what events lay outside of this period. Overall, the time periods allotted to conduct a comprehensive investigation into events involving mass human rights violations appeared far too short (on average, between three and six weeks). Only a few reports included a reference to the rationale behind the limited timeframe of the mission, the limited time in the country, as well as the effect the accelerated timeframe had on the inquiry. Most reports did not make such rationale or limitation explicit, thus it was impossible to determine if the length of time allotted for an inquiry was related to outside factors, such as insufficient funding or the lack of cooperation of non-consenting subject States, or was related to the discernment of the commissioners.

Facts Alleged and Conclusions Reached

With regard to including comprehensive information about the facts alleged in the investigation, and how these led to conclusions reached, 27 of the reports (87%) included a comprehensive summary of the facts within the report, 30 of the reports (96.7%) included a comprehensive description of the human rights violations involved, yet only eight reports (25.8%) included statements about the submission of the evidence. All reports included statements establishing the facts surrounding the issues involved, and all reports included information on the conclusions reached in the investigation.

While most reports included at least a brief description of the facts alleged, noting which allegations were deemed valid, overall the reports varied widely from vague statements about allegations of human rights abuses to specific lists of the facts alleged. Also, most reports provided fairly specific information about the facts that the commission established to be valid and did a generally adequate job of tying together the facts established regarding the human rights violated with the conclusions reached. The Bahrain Commission report, and the Report of the United Nations Fact-finding Mission on the Gaza Conflict ("Gaza Conflict Commission") provided the most comprehensive information in this regard (e.g., facts alleged, facts established and conclusions reached) compared to the other reports reviewed.

Investigative Methodology

With regard to the investigative methodology used during the fact-finding missions, the reports varied significantly in terms of the ways in which the investigations were carried out, rendering replication impossible in many cases. Approximately half the reports included a section on methodology used, with varying levels of detail,[46] with the remaining reports including no explicit information on investigative methodology used, despite several reports stating that a 'high standard of methodology' was used.

With regard to whether information about the explicit methodology used in the investigation was included in the report, 20 of the reports (64.5%) failed to include this information, including how the investigation was generally carried out, information about the origin of evidence relied upon in the investigation, what specific evidence was evaluated, and what methods were used to evaluate the evidence. While eleven reports (35.4%) did include a "methodology" section, the majority of these sections were quite brief and failed to include explicit information on how the investigators obtained and vetted evidence, including evidence that influenced outcomes. The Bahrain Commission was the exception to this pattern in that the final COI report included comprehensive information regarding all aspects of evidence origin, management, and vetting, including the qualifications of those experts who evaluated the nature of, and credibility of the evidence.

Evidence Management

With regard to evidence management, very few reports included information on the type of database used to store data, such as tracking witnesses and evidence reviewed. The majority of reports did not appear to comply with standard methods used in criminal investigations or research studies (e.g., the scientific method, qualitative or quantitative methodology), even when such standards have been in existence for quite some time, and are accepted in various fields of inquiry. For instance, despite many of the reports including claims that high methodological standards were employed, statements of fact that were relied upon particularly related to socio-political context failed to include citation support reflecting reliance on scholarly sources. It appears that in most reports, exceptionally high value was placed on eyewitness testimony, despite the lack of empirical support for eyewitness reliability. Some reports referenced triangulation of the data, but only cited two sources of evidence, both of which involved eyewitness. Very few reports included information on how investigators or experts recorded direct observations (e.g., note-taking, memory, etc.).

---

[46] Reports with an easily identifiable section on methodology included: Chile Commission, Gaza Commission, Gaza Flotilla Commission, Libya Commission, Rwanda Commission, Cambodia Commission, Burundi Commission, Yugoslavia Commission, Bahrain Commission, Pakistan Commission, South Vietnam Commission.

Few reports included any substantive information about the standards of proof employed, the chain of custody, how evidence was evaluated as credible (or determined to be non-credible), and preserved and kept secured. For instance, most reports were not explicit in terms of how evidence was obtained and how it was handled once it was obtained. Additionally, most reports had only limited information about physical sites accessed (e.g. hospitals, refugee camps, detention camps, prisons, military installations), the nature of the sites and how they were inspected. Very few of the reports included information about fact-checking or vetting of evidence. Related to this issue is the vetting of experts who were often responsible for determining what was and was not deemed relevant and credible evidence (or what the evidence indicated in relation to possible human rights abuses), including what qualifications they possessed and what criteria was used to deem them experts within a particular discipline.

For example, the Report of the High Commissioner on OHCHR's visit to Yemen ("Yemen Commission") indicates that "over 6000 pages of documents, 160 compact discs, 6000 photographs, and 1800 videos" were obtained and reviewed by commissioners, however the report does not provide any substantive information on how this evidence was vetted, what portions of this evidence was utilized, and who evaluated this evidence. Another example of poor documentation regarding the vetting of evidence by the Yemen Commission includes a factual assertion contained in the COI report regarding the commission's documentation of weaponry use (p. 8), without providing clarity about who was responsible for the verification and documentation (a commissioner, weapons expert, etc.), and whether the documenting party was sufficiently qualified to determine the nature of weaponry usage.

While most reports could have included more comprehensive information about the evidence obtained from witnesses and its management, the reports that did provide a relatively comprehensive list of evidence with a description of the chain of evidence were the 'Report of the International Commission of Inquiry on Libya' ("Libya Commission"); the Bahrain Commission report; the 'International Commission of Inquiry established under resolution 1012 (1995) concerning Burundi' ("Burundi Commission"); the 'Report of the United Nations Fact-Finding Mission to South Vietnam' ("South Vietnam Commission"), and the Guinea Commission report. In fact, the Guinea Commission report explicitly stated that all evidence of wrongdoing was subjected to double verification, stating:

In fulfillment of its mandate, the Commission decided that in order to obtain the quality of evidence needed to establish the facts, the information received must be checked against independent sources, preferably eyewitness accounts, and independently verified evidence assembled to demonstrate that a person may reasonably be suspected of having participated in the commission of a crime. This is the approach commonly used by international commissions of inquiry, which endeavor to put together reliable evidence corroborated by verified testimony. Thus, the report does not include any testimony that has not been corroborated by at least one other source and the statistics on the various types of violations refer only to individuals who have been identified by name" (Guinea Commission, p. 9).

Relevant Contextual Information

Very few reports provided comprehensive information with regard to the historical, socio-political and geographical context of the conflict that often resulted in mass human rights violations. Some reports did include a summary of relevant context in an impartial manner, with some reports even including maps of alleged human rights violations. With regard to the influence of external actors, only the Bahrain Commission and the Burundi Commission included substantive information in this regard, despite the fact that virtually all COIs involved regional conflicts with external actors. For example, the 'Report of the Independent Inquiry into the Actions of the United Nations during the 1994 Genocide in Rwanda' failed to include information on the historical-socio-political context in relation to the civil war and subsequent genocide, including the role that external actors within the Belgian and French governments played in the civil war and genocide, which may have influenced how the United Nations responded to the genocide (which was the focus of the inquiry).

Other examples of COI reports failing to include relevant context includes the Côte d'Ivoire Commission report, which provided a brief description of the country's recent history, including the disputed election and the international community's support for the Outtara government, but did not provide more comprehensive contextual information, particularly in relation to its relatively recent independence from French colonization. Nor did the report include information on the ongoing substantial role of French mining conglomerates in the country's economic and political developments. Similarly, the Report of the United Nations High Commission for Human Rights on the violation of human rights in Honduras since the coup d'état on 28 June 2009 ("Honduras Commission")failed to reference the role the United States is alleged to have played in the conflict that resulted in the coup d'état (the focus of the investigation).

Report Compilation

There were dramatic differences in how the COI reports were compiled, with very little, if any consistency from report to report. A comparison of the reports revealed a lack of consistency in section, report flow, and even report length. For instance, the reports ranged from 16 to 575 pages, with an average length of the reports being 95 pages, with a standard deviation of 143 pages, reflecting a very broad range of report lengths. In the shorter reports, no references were made as to the reasons for their brevity, including why seemingly important sections (such as 'methodology') were omitted.

Commissioners and Mission Personnel

With regard to the hiring and management of COI personnel (commissioners, staff and experts), 26 of the reports (84%) included the number of commissioners appointed to the investigation, and 24 of the reports (77.4%) included the commissioners' names somewhere within the report (although in most of the reports the names were not easily found and a considerable amount of effort was exerted to locate all of the Commissioners' names). The only report that included comprehensive information about COI personnel, including the names of commissions and their curriculum vitas, was the Bahrain Commission's report. Finally, seven of the reports (22.5%) included no information about the appointed commissioners whatsoever.

The average number of commissioners appointed among the reports in the sample was about four, with a standard deviation of 1.6 (median of 3.5/mode of three), and a range between one and seven. Among the reports that did include information about the appointed Commissioners, only two reports (6.5%) indicated that the appointed Commissioners signed a 'Code of Conduct' agreement,[47] with the remaining 29 reports (93.5%) making no reference to whether a 'Code of Conduct' report was signed. With regard to COI staff, only five reports (16.1%) referenced the actual number of staff hired, with no report including names of all staff members, or whether COI staff signed a 'Code of Conduct' agreement. Only two reports (6.5%) included the total number of experts hired.[48] The 2005 Darfur Commission report was the only one that indicated whether conflict of interest check for

---

[47] 'Report of the International Commission of Inquiry for Togo' ("Togo Commission"), and the Bahrain Commission report.
[48] 'Report of the International Commission of Inquiry on Darfur to the United Nations Secretary General Pursuant to Security Council Resolution 1564 of 18 September 2004' ("2005 Darfur Commission") and the Bahrain Commission report.

commissioners had been conducted, with the remaining reports including no reference as to whether appointed or assigned personnel were subject to conflict of interest checks.

In general, the majority of the reports failed to include identifying information about the commissioners, interpreters, investigators, experts or staff working on a mission, including names, nationalities and qualifications. In fact, several reports made no reference to staff whatsoever, and the majority of those that did reference staff included no information about the roles they played in the investigation. Very few reports referenced whether evidence, including witness testimony, was translated, as well as the backgrounds of the interpreters. With regard to how translations were managed, while the majority of reports failed to make any reference to the vetting of interpreters, or how interpretations were managed, the Rwanda Commission report was an exception, having done an excellent job of describing the methodology of selecting interpreters as well as how translations were managed, referencing the sensitive nature of hiring interpreters, and checking translations for accuracy, noting the ethnic nature of the conflict that resulted in the conflict, and in genocide.[49]

With regard time spent in the country and/or region, the majority of the reports were very unclear about which personnel visited the country, and which did not,[50] making it impossible to determine whether the commissioners actually visited the country, or whether staff were the only commission personnel in the region. A clear exception to this was the Bahrain Commission report, which made explicit which the commissioners, chair, and staff remained in the country, and for what duration. The Bahrain Commission report also provided the names, nationalities, and biographies of all commissioners, as well as an organizational chart and a listing of the quantity of each type of personnel, (but did not provide names of staff and/ or experts, nor information about the vetting of personnel). Similarly, the Chilean Commission report, the names of all Commissioners and staff members, as well as a listing of their respective roles were included. With regard to experts used though, the majority of the reports failed to include the qualifications of experts, including what criteria were used to evaluate experts' credentials.

---

[49] Commissioners subjected all evidence to multiple translations from both ethnic groups to ensure that there was consistency in translations.

[50] See the Togo Commission report, the Kenya Commission reports, the 'Report of the Commission of Inquiry on Lebanon pursuant to Human Rights Council resolution S-2/1' ("Lebanon Commission"), the Guinea Commission, and the 'Report of the United Nations High Commission for Human Rights on the violation of human rights in Honduras since the coup d'état on 28 June 2009' ("Honduras Commission").

Additionally there appeared to be no consistent use of particular titles of COI personnel, both within reports, as well as between reports, with titles frequently being interchanged, contributing to the potential for significant confusion. For instance, the 2005 Darfur Commission report includes a reference to the budget not allowing for more than 13 experts, but the report does not make clear that 13 experts were ultimately hired. In a subsequent section the report notes that there were 13 members in the "investigative team", yet it is unclear whether the "investigative team" was also considered "experts". To further add to the lack of clarity, the report provides specific titles for those on the investigative team, stating that "the Commission's investigation team was led by a Chief Investigator and included four investigators, two female investigators specializing in gender violence, four forensic experts and two military analysts,"[51] thus it appears as though the report writer is using the terms "investigative team", "investigator", "expert", and "analyst" interchangeably, not only leading to lacking clarity with regard to role differentiation in the 2005 Darfur COI mission, but also rendering cross-mission comparisons very difficult.

Witnesses, Victims and Detainees

With regard to witnesses and victims, most reports included insufficient information on how interviews were structured and facilitated, including what questions were asked, whether forensic interviewing techniques were used (if any), how statements were translated, and how witnesses were vetted. Only five of the reports (16.1%) in the sample included explicit methodology on how investigative interviews with witnesses and victims were conducted,[52] with the remaining 26 reports (84%) including no reference whatsoever to interview methodology. With regard to whether investigative teams were able to access all witnesses and victims, twenty-seven of the reports (87%) noted that investigators were granted access to victims and witnesses. Sixteen of the reports (51.6%) included some reference to whether the investigators were granted access to detainees, but

---

[51] 2005 Darfur Commission report, 13.
[52] The reports that included interview methodology were: 'The Study of Reported Violations of Human Rights in Chile, with Particular Reference to Torture and other Cruel, Inhuman or Degrading Treatment or Punishment", "Report of the Commission of Inquiry on the Reported Massacres in Mozambique", "Report of the Mission to Kyrgyzstan by the Office of the High Commissioner of Human Rights concerning the Killings in Andijan, Uzbekistan of 13–14 May 2005", "Bahrain Independent Commission of Inquiry", and "Report of the United Nations Fact-Finding Mission to South Vietnam").

the reference was not definitive regarding whether they were barred from accessing other witnesses and victims. Twelve reports (38.7%) noted that commissioners were granted access to detainees, and four reports (12.9%) noted that access to detainees was not granted. The remaining 15 reports (48.3%) did not include any reference to whether or not the investigative team was granted access to detainees.

With regard to confidentiality and security of witnesses and victims, only seven of the reports (22.5%) included specific references to interviewing witnesses and victims in private, with six reports (19.4%) noting that witnesses were interviewed privately and one report (3.1%) noting that they were not. Only seven reports (22.6%) referenced information on providing for the protection of witnesses and victims, with six of these seven reports (19.4%) stating that witnesses and victims were offered protection, and the remaining report (3.1%) stating they were not. The remaining 24 reports (77.4%) did not make any reference to protecting witnesses and victims either in the affirmative or negative.

With regard to whether the investigative team was granted access to all relevant physical sites, such as hospitals, schools, prisons and other sites where violations were alleged to have occurred, 21 of the reports (67.7%) made some reference to whether or not the investigative team was granted access, and of these 10 reports (32.2%) noted that the team was granted access to all relevant sites, and 11 reports (35.6%) noted they were not. The remaining 10 reports (32.2%) did not make reference either way as to whether investigators had access to all sites.

In many reports no information was referenced at all with regard to who the witnesses and victims were, whether they have been vetted, or how the vetting occurred. The majority of reports did not specify how the information was obtained from the witnesses and victims, thus it was impossible to determine whether the information obtained from witnesses and victims was obtained from personal interviews, written statements, whether the information was obtained first-hand, or second-hand (i.e., from NGOs). For example, a report might note that the Commissioners heard testimony from private individuals, but the report might not clarify whether or how the testimony was recorded and what was done with those recordings if any were obtained, or how they were protected. Additionally, most reports were not explicit about whether there were groups of witnesses, victims, and/or detainees with whom they did not have access. Some exceptions were the Bahrain Commission report, which provided explicit information that all parties were available for interviews, the 'Report of the Independent Expert of the Commission on Human Rights on the Situation of Human

Rights in Afghanistan' ("Afghanistan Commission") which noted that the Commission had access to all sites and detainees controlled by the Afghan government, but not to those controlled by the United States, and the Côte d'Ivoire Commission, which noted that the Ouattara government allowed the Commissioners relatively unimpeded access to areas controlled by Gbagbo forces, but were not permitted to examine alleged mass graves, interview prisoners, or even talk with the general population. Overall, the majority of reports failed to include information about power dynamics in the region, and whether or not limitations were placed upon the Commissioners, or the impact these limitations may have had on the investigation.

The majority of reports also provided very little if any information on the vetting of witnesses, victims and detainees for possible conflicts of interest, level of credibility, possible political agendas, or any possible bias, thus it was impossible to determine whether the Commissioners and/or investigators attempted to evaluate whether statements were proffered as a result of a hidden agenda, as a result of bias, or were a result of bribery or blackmail.[53] For instance, in the Report of the International Commission of Inquiry for Togo ("Togo Commission"), it was noted that most of the witnesses contacted in Cotonou (Benin) were bribed to give false information, which clearly affected the credibility of the statements. The inclusion of this information in the COI report would have yielded valuable insights into the veracity of witness statements, and how Commissioners managed these types of situations. Further, in regard to the COI reports that specified evidence obtained from government officials (e.g., military, government ministers, etc.) the names of government officials were not included. This is particularly relevant information, especially because the information was obtained from officials in governments that were the subject of the investigation.

The majority of reports did not specify any substantive information about the witnesses or victims they interviewed, including the interview methodology used, including who facilitated the interviews and whether the interviewers were trained in forensic interviewing techniques. Further, the majority of the reports did not include the conditions under which witnesses and victims were interviewed, providing no information about whether interviews were private and confidential, whether informed consent was provided, whether other investigators were in the room at the time of the interview, the location where the interviews took place, or the nature of the interview (i.e., structured with prepared questions, semi-structured

---

[53] Some reviewers questioned whether witnesses and those identifying themselves as victims were possibly members of the former regime, but this information was impossible to determine from the information contained in a majority of the reports.

or open-ended, one-on-one, group, whether the witnesses and victims were interviewed in private, whether there was an advocate, such as a counselor or social worker present, who was present in the room during the interview, etc.).

Additionally, in some reports, eyewitness accounts were presented as 'alleged',[54] while in other reports the term 'alleged' in reference to eyewitness accounts was not included,[55] leading to confusion regarding whether the use of the term 'alleged' implied the need for increased scrutiny of validity of witness accounts, or whether the omission of the term 'alleged' in regard to eyewitness testimony implies some level of bias on the part of the Commissioners. Since all witness and victim statements are considered alleged until conclusions are reached, consistently using the term 'alleged' in reference to eyewitness testimony would increase clarity across all COI reports. Moreover, only a few reports included the total number of witnesses and victims interviewed,[56] and in some reports, the breakdowns of witnesses, victims and detainees interviewed did not match the total number provided.

Finally, with regard to the protection of witnesses, victims and detainees, the majority of reports included no information regarding the protection of witnesses and victims. The reports that did reference protection did not include substantive information about how this process occurred, and whether it extended beyond the timeframe of the inquiry. Thus it was impossible to determine the nature and scope of the protection offered (solely during the interviews, throughout the mission, or after the mission ended). For instance, only the Bahrain Commission report made specific reference to providing for both confidentiality and security of witnesses and victims, although no information in that regard as to how, or for how long the protection and security of witnesses and victims was provided.

The Role of Non-Governmental Organizations

Very few of the reports made the role of NGOs in obtaining witness and victim statements (or other evidence) explicit. In the reports that did reference that some witness and victim statements were provided by NGOs, there was often no information provided regarding steps taken, such as a tracking system, to ensure that such evidence was not duplicative of the information obtained directly by the COI team (i.e., whether the witness statements provided by NGOs were the same witnesses interviewed by the

---

[54] See Togo Commission and Honduras Commission reports.
[55] See Beit Hanoun Commission and Gaza Conflict Commission reports.
[56] See the Bahrain Commission report.

commissioners/investigators). Further, no report that referenced working in collaboration with an NGO provided information about the vetting of the NGO, or the information they provided, in order to evaluate possible conflicts of interest, such as a political agendas or previously demonstrated bias. For example, in the original Libya Commission report (A/HRC/17/44) there were references to several NGOs that played significant roles in providing witness and victim testimony as well as information on human rights violations perpetrated by then President Muamar Al Qadhafi (the primary subject of the investigation). Yet at least two of the NGOs cited were owned and developed by immediate family members of Qadhafi (his wife and daughter), who were also accused of alleged human rights violations. In the subsequently released edited report (A/HRC/19/68) all references to NGO collaboration had been removed, yet no mention was made as to whether the implications of the collaboration was addressed, or whether the information provided by the NGOs was still a part of the evidence relied upon in reaching conclusions. Additionally, while most reports stated that the Libya Commission received information from various media outlets, the names of the media outlets were not provided, rendering vetting for possible conflicts of interest impossible. For instance, it was impossible to determine whether the media outlets and journalists had taken sides in the conflict, thus acting in an advocacy role, either in support of the actors being investigated (i.e., state-run media), or in support of rebel groups or non-state actors.

Recommendations and Follow-up

The nature of recommendations made by commissioners varied significantly. For instance, some reports included recommendations regarding victims' needs, while many reports did not. Some recommendations were far too brief or abstract to be put into action, while others were more comprehensive and concrete. Further, most reports failed to establish a relationship between conclusions of human rights violated, and recommendations, including any follow-up action. For instance, some reports included recommendations of reparations in response to mass human rights violations, but failed to follow up to ensure that victims had been compensated. Other reports failed to make obvious recommendations related to accountability for governments (and members of governments) when the COI determined that egregious behavior had occurred. For instance, the Togo Commission report included credible information about government-sponsored bribes to district heads, journalists, fishermen and other witnesses in Benin for the purposes of influencing the outcome of the inquiry, and yet the report did not include any recommendations in terms of how to address this issue, nor did the report include recommendations regarding the arrest and prosecution of former Prime Minister, Agbeyome' Kodjo, for his alleged support of militiamen who abducted and raped women.

Budgets and Resource Allocation
The only report among all those reviewed that included any substantive information about the budget for the COI, including how the resources were allocated, and whether the budget was audited, and made public was the Bahrain Commission report. The only other report that contained any reference to a budget was the South Vietnam Commission report, which included the amount of the COI budget, but no additional information of a substantive nature that could have yielded information about whether the COI was appropriately financially supported, and whether the budget was managed appropriately.

Discussion on the Challenges in Implementing and Facilitating Fact-Finding Missions

There are numerous challenges investigative bodies face when planning, implementing and facilitating MRF missions, particularly fact-finding missions, many of which are explored in the literature. For instance, fact-finding missions are most often carried out in regions wrought with cyclical violence, many missions are often poorly funded thus mission personnel are frequently in the position of attempting to accomplish monumental tasks with minimal resources, and often in the face of insufficient regional cooperation. Yet in addition to the challenges inherent in any investigative process under often dire circumstances, a considerable number of challenges arise from other factors as well, often related to the political nature of the UN, whereas referenced earlier, results of fact-finding missions are far too often driven by the political will and interests of powerful UN Member States.[57]

International law scholars have also noted challenges that arise when mission personnel exceed the boundaries of their mandates, and when investigations and reporting are inconsistent or irregular due to

---

[57] Bassiouni, "Appraising UN-justice"; HPCR Working Paper.

the lack of any universally adopted standardized procedures dictating how investigations should be conducted. In fact, the lack of an accepted methodological framework leads to inconsistencies in any number of investigative components, including unequal resource allocation, irregularities in the application of standards of proof, inconsistencies in the selection and training of personnel, mismanagement of witnesses and victims, and an increased potential for bias in the evaluation of evidence. Challenges, regardless of their origin, must be anticipated (and appropriately addressed) due to the unwieldy nature of investigating alleged human rights violations arising out of conflict situations. Perhaps Bailey put it best when in reference to the complex and challenging nature of fact-finding missions, he stated, "the difficulty about facts is that there are so many of them."[58]

Mandates and Terms of Reference

The results of this study show that there is consistent variation in how mandates are drafted, with a general lack of transparency. The lack of transparency in how mandates were drafted and interpreted, as well as how much of this process was included in the COI reports ranged considerably from report to report. For instance, some reports included both the mandates exactly as they were reflected in the UN resolution, as well as the commissioner interpretation of the mandate, and some reports included considerably less information. The mandate and terms of reference dictate the parameters of the mission, as well as its objectives, thus the transparency in the process of the development and interpretation of the mandate is one of the primary ways that fact-finding missions can be effectively facilitated as well as evaluated.

Many of the challenges related to the implementation and facilitation of fact-finding missions relate to poorly constructed mandates and/or ambiguous interpretations, which can lead to numerous problems including investigative irregularities and biased results. For instance, a challenge noted in the literature relates to the tendency for boundaries to become blurred between various types of MRF activities, where unclear mandates, or investigator confusion leads to missions that exceed their prescribed parameters, such as when a monitoring or reporting mission is facilitated as if it were a fact-finding mission. The HPCR report cites the example of the 'Mapping Exercise in the Democratic Republic of the Congo,' a reporting mission that was treated as a fact-finding mission by some of the investigators,

---

[58] Sydney D. Bailey. "UN Fact-Finding and Human Rights Complaints," *International Affairs (Royal Institute of International Affairs 1944-)* 48, no. 2 (1972): 250.

which according to UN personnel, caused unnecessary expenditures in both time and resources.[59] Highlighting the problematic nature of unclear boundaries and exceeded mandates in MRF activities, the HPCR report cautions that when mandates are exceeded relationships with target countries may be put in jeopardy, particularly when monitors or reporters act as fact-finders, thus stepping out of their supportive and advisory roles and into the role of investigators. One way of ensuring that COI activities remain within their prescribed boundaries and meet the mandate objectives intended by the mandate drafters is through the development of mandates that reflect clarity and easily interpreted objectives.

Lack of Standardized Methodology Guiding Fact-Finding Missions

The results of this study support the consensus in the literature that international fact-finding missions, particularly those implemented by the UN, do not reflect the use of a uniform and standardized methodological framework for the implementation and facilitation of investigations, either with regard to how the investigations are facilitated, or with how the reports are compiled. While a few of the COI reports analyzed had some information on investigative methodology, the overwhelming majority did not. The absence of standardized methodology renders the analysis of a fact-finding mission very challenging since it is difficult to determine whether deficits existed in the investigation approach, in the report compilation, or both. For instance, while some of the fact-finding missions may have employed appropriately high methodological standards, it would be impossible to determine this if information in this regard is not included in the final COI report.[60]

A fact-finding mission mandate determines *what* evidence is to be gathered by the investigative team, while the investigative methodology determines the *ways* in which evidence is to be gathered and *how* it is to be analyzed.[61] Thus the issue of universal and standardized investigative methodological standards relates essentially to all variables explored in the present study. Despite the UN acknowledging the need for a standardized framework for guiding fact-finding investigative processes as early as

---

[59] Micaela Frulli, "Fact-finding or Paving the Road to Criminal Justice? Some Reflections on United Nations Commissions of Inquiry" *Journal of International Criminal Justice* 10, (2012): 1323–1338; Bassiouni, "Appraising UN-justice"; HPCR Working Paper.
[60] Ibid.
[61] HPCR Working Paper.

1968,[62] to date the UN has not formally adopted a standard investigative methodology. In fact, numerous scholars and UN observers have noted how the lack of any type of standard operating procedure to guide fact-finding missions contributes to a rather disjointed and haphazard approach to data gathering and analysis by the range of UN entities engaging in fact-finding activities.[63] While the UN and NGO community have developed various manuals on fact-finding methodology,[64] no uniform framework has been accepted as authoritative.[65] Boutruche asserts that international human rights fact-finding missions should have standards as high as any government investigation, which is required to be "thorough, complete, independent, impartial, and technically competent."[66]

The lack of any standardization in methodological approaches to fact-finding missions creates problems in establishing an appropriate standard of proof relative to the type of mission, which can lead to the misapplication of evidence (i.e., to a higher level than was intended). This is particularly relevant in light of the increased reliance on fact-finding investigations in bringing perpetrators to justice in criminal proceedings. If fact-finding missions, particularly COIs, are not subject to a universally accepted standard of proof, conclusions cannot be substantiated with any level of confidence. Additionally, the lack of training in criminal law among those most commonly responsible for establishing fact-finding bodies, as well as those responsible for investigating alleged violations of international humanitarian law, has the potential of negatively affecting every aspect of the evidence gathering process.[67] For example, the goal of a fact-finding mission is to "determine the most effective route for ensuring

---

[62] Bailey notes that a proposal for a "well defined rules of procedure for the orderly and efficient discharge of their functions by the United Nations bodies concerned with the field of human rights" was approved at the Tehran Conference on Human Rights, and yet the final draft issued by the Security-General's revised draft was significantly watered down, according to Bailey, stipulating primarily that UN bodies conducting fact-finding missions should visit the regions where the alleged violations occurred and collect information, 266.

[63] Robertson, "Human Rights and Fact Finding".

[64] See Lund-London Guidelines on International Human Rights Fact-Finding Visits and Reports for an example of a framework developed by an NGO for NGO-facilitated fact-finding missions.

[65] HPCR Working Paper, 8.

[66] Theo Boutruche, "Credible Fact-Finding and Allegations of International Humanitarian Law Violations: Challenges in Theory and Practice", *Journal of Conflict & Security Law*, 16 no. 1, (2011): 105–140.

[67] M. Cherif Bassiouni. "Former Yugoslavia: Investigating Violations of International Humanitarian Law and Establishing an International Criminal Tribunal. Security Dialogue," 25 (1994): 409.

accountability,"[68] and as such fact-finding missions are not equivalent to a formal judicial process, thus the standard of evidence is not as rigorous as would be required in a criminal investigation. Despite the lower level of evidentiary requirements, fact-finding missions are increasingly relied upon in criminal court proceedings, or are relied upon to make recommendations to the mandating body regarding the prosecution of alleged perpetrators, which can lead to the misapplication of evidence, faulty conclusions and compromised criminal accountability.[69] Fulli cites this very issue when he states:

> These are not the most solid grounds on which credible criminal prosecutions may be based. Indeed many reports issued by fact-finding commissions expressly state that 'the findings do not attempt to identify the individuals responsible for the commission of offences nor do they pretend to reach the standard of proof applicable in criminal trials'. Yet in many cases these reports represent the basis of allegations leading to criminal prosecution.[70]

The lack any universal standards for how fact-finding missions are to be conducted not only leads to lack of clarity with regard to the roles, functions, and parameters of each type of MRF mission, but also leads to confusion in how fact-finding investigative activities are to be facilitated, as well as to how the reports are to be compiled. One fact-finding investigator referenced in an HCPR report advocates for increased accountability and the establishment of a minimum standard, noting that it is unacceptable to "send people in unprepared, making it up as they go along."[71] Essentially, the lack of any standardized methodological framework for guiding the inquiry process often results in the utilization of flawed methodology, which in turn leads to incorrect conclusions, and compromised relationships with Member States. One of the most serious consequences of this challenge is the potential for a significant negative effect on victims of international human rights abuses. Frulli captures the comprehensive nature of this dynamic, stating:

The absence of applicable standards 'means that there is no basis to test the validity of the research in order to assess the plausibility of the conclusions. It is safe to say that no scientific research methodology would consider the [current] approach as anything but selective, insufficient, unreliable, and, at best, anecdotal'.[72]

---

[68] Ibid., 13.
[69] Frulli, "Fact-finding or Paving the Road".
[70] Ibid.
[71] Ibid., 42.
[72] Frulli, "Fact-finding or Paving the Road", 1326.

Currently, methodology for the most part tends to be mission driven, with each mission determining what methodology works best for its specific context. While this approach offers necessary flexibility and may support the unique nature of each mission, it does not address the need for uniform methods for approaching such issues as hiring and training of appropriate personnel including investigators, vetting of experts and witnesses, the use of forensic interviewing techniques, and standards of proof appropriate for various types of fact-finding activities. HCPR emphasizes that one key way of addressing the issue of inconsistent methodological standards to guide fact-finding activities is to conduct empirical research on the effect and effectiveness of various methodological approaches, which will not only fill current knowledge gaps, but will also assist in the development of standardized systems that address past mistakes.[73]

Commissioners and Personnel

The results of this study reveal in large part that the hiring of commissioners and mission personnel (i.e., staff, experts, etc.) is not a transparent process, as the majority of reports did not include comprehensive background information on hiring practices, including what criteria was used for the hiring of various types of personnel, whether conflicts of interest checks were conducted (to ensure impartiality and objectivity), or whether a Code of Conduct agreement was established and implemented. Thus, it was impossible to evaluate whether criteria for various types of experts (munitions experts, for instance) was consistent across various missions, as well as whether missions effectively managed internal and external influences and pressures (without seeking data from outside sources). In this regard, the results of this study are far more an analysis of what information was included in the COI reports, than an analysis of the actual hiring and training practices of the mission commissioners and personnel. For instance, the absence of information about conflicts of interest checks being conducted on mission personnel, including commissioners, experts and staff, in the fact-finding mission report, does not necessarily indicate that none existed.

Transparency in hiring practices used in international fact-finding missions is vital to ensuring that the values of truth and justice, based upon impartiality and objectivity, are upheld. Despite these foundational values, Bassiouni notes that far too often hiring of staff, including department heads

---

[73] HPCR Working Paper.

and experts in fact-finding missions, are politically motivated.[74] This is not a new phenomenon, as Bailey expressed this very same caution over four decades ago in his article on common complaints about UN fact-finding missions. Bailey cited several problems that ensued when UN reporting on alleged human rights abuses were one-sided, which he asserted was frequently the case. According to Bailey, such one-sided reporting often led to political problems with subject States, including reduced cooperation, interference with the investigation to influence outcomes, and refusal or withdrawal of consent. In describing this dynamic, Bailey stated:

> UN fact-finding organs should be constituted on an equitable and representative basis and not composed simply of known opponents of the situation to be investigated…It is true that if a fact-finding body is composed of like-minded members, it will probably accomplish its task more quickly than if it contains within its membership some of the many conflicts and disputes which have been brought to the United Nations for resolution. An *esprit de corps* will quickly develop, and it will not be necessary to argue about first principles. But the easiest and fastest procedure may not necessarily be in the long-term interests of the United Nations and its members: a partisan report may make it easier to pursue an immediate political objective, but the effect is to discredit the Organization and to encourage states against whom complaints are made to behave obstructively.

Thus while it might be tempting to staff a UN fact-finding mission with personnel who all share the same preconceived notions about a situation or conflict, such a practice will risk relationships, discredit the UN, and potentially increase the risk of conflict in the subject region.

Robertson echoes Bassiouni and Bailey's cautions noting the propensity for some regional experts to have already made up their minds about a situation. In order to avoid the issue of pre-judgment, Robertson recommends securing experts who "have no connection at all with the country or the persons involved in the mission, but who have a reputation for good judgment."[75] HCRP acknowledges the risk of hiring regional experts with pre-conceived notions about a conflict, and "a past that might be offensive to the country", but cautions that hiring someone with no background in

---

[74] Ibid., 263.
[75] Geoffrey Robertson, "Human Rights and Fact Finding: Some Legal and Ethical Dilemmas, Human Rights Institute, Thematic Paper No 1", *International Bar Association*, (June 2009): 7.

a region can have the same effect – placing the legitimacy of the mission at risk.[76]

The challenge of hiring experts for human rights investigations who are regional experts with a demonstrated ability to remain objective and impartial requires increased focus on "transparency and consultation with multiple stakeholders".[77] An example of a newer system that attempts to address this challenge is one adopted in 2007 by the HRC for Special Procedure mandates (a human rights monitoring mechanism). HRC's newly adopted system involves the selection of candidates from a public list prepared by the OHCHR, generated from nominated candidates who are subsequently approved by a group of diplomats from each region. Piccone notes that criteria for appointment include "human rights expertise and experience in the field of the mandate, independence, impartiality, personal integrity, and objectivity."[78] Once the OHCHR process for approval is complete, the list is presented to the HRC for final approval. Piccone asserts that this new method for approving and appointing human rights experts has been successful in facilitating the development of a diverse pool of experts from every region, consequently reducing the practice of "backroom dealings and manipulation, inherent in the old system".[79]

While this new system has to date not been evaluated empirically, (thus it remains uncertain whether the stated values of independence, impartiality and personal integrity, are any more effectively supported than in the former, more directive system), it does serve as an example of an attempt to address the challenges of balancing the need for regional expertise, while upholding the values of objectivity and impartiality. Whether such a system would be effective in COIs as well, would also need to be subjected to empirical examination as well.

Witnesses, Victims and Detainees

The results of this study revealed that information on the manner in which witnesses, victims and detainees were managed ranged significantly from report to report, and likely from mission to mission. Very few reports included any substantive information on interviewing methodology, rendering it impossible to effectively evaluate the reliability of evidence

---

[76] HPCR Working Paper, 40.
[77] Ted Piccone, *"Catalysts for Change: How the UN's Independent Experts Promote Human Rights"* (Washington, DC: The Brookings Institute, 2012): 3.
[78] Ibid., 3.
[79] Ibid., 4.

obtained from oral and/or written testimony. Further, the majority of reports failed to include substantive information on the origin of eyewitness testimony (i.e., direct, through a third source, such as an NGO, etc.), thus the credibility of such testimony in most missions evaluated was unclear.

In addition to the credibility and reliability of witness and victim testimony is the issue of witness, victim and detainee security and protection. Very few of the COI reports reviewed referenced the issue of security and protection of witnesses and victims who cooperated with the investigation, and those reports that did reference this issue, failed to provide any substantive information regarding how these tasks were accomplished, or even how "protection" was defined (e.g., physical, psychological, etc.). Thus, it was difficult to render any assessment with regard to whether sufficient and appropriate protection offered (if any), and whether the protection offered met best practice standards for both physical and psychological protection of witnesses and victims in trauma situations (i.e., limiting the potential for re-traumatization).

Boutruche cites the importance of consistently applying a minimum standard of proof in order for evidence to be considered 'verifiable', which in UN fact-finding missions typically includes at least one primary source and at least two additional supporting sources.[80] Boutruche also notes the vital importance of fact-finding bodies relying on a wide range of sources in order to ensure a balanced investigation, where various perspectives are sought, so that opposing viewpoints can be resolved. In the process of obtaining a wide range of witness statements, it is vitally important to utilize a rigorous standard of proof. In UN fact-finding missions the most commonly relied upon source of evidence is witness testimony, despite the general unreliable nature of such evidence, due to the tendency for eyewitnesses of traumatic events to be influenced by personal bias, intimidation, and the consequences of trauma. Baily noted the "inherent difficulties in the proof of allegations of torture or ill-treatment" for a variety of reasons, including a victim's fear of reprisal, victim allegations based upon "distortions, exaggerations, or false perceptions" rooted in anti-government propaganda, even detainee denial and embellishment for the purposes of self-vindication in the eyes of "co-accused and political friends".[81]

For instance, with regard to credibility factors, Robertson warns human rights fact-finders to be very cautious when evaluating the veracity

---

[80] See Boutruche, "Credible Fact-Finding", 114.
[81] Sydney Bailey. (1972). UN Fact-Finding and Human Rights Complaints. International Affairs (Royal Institute of International Affairs 1944-) 48, no. 2 (1972): 262.

of witness disclosures due to those witnesses who have "an axe to grind", or are motivated by "blind partisanship", stating:

> ...they have undoubtedly suffered and will be anxious to emphasize the guilt of those they believe (or have been made to believe) are to blame. Fact finders must also factor in the motive that many witnesses have to exaggerate or to emphasize their own innocence: when claiming refugee status, or hoping to claim such status, they will have a motive to exaggerate the extent of their persecution, especially if they think the fact- finders' report may subsequently assist their asylum claim. Always ask: *cui bono?* (who benefits?)[82]

One way of managing witness testimony is through the utilization of scientifically based interviewing techniques when interviewing witnesses and victims of violent crime.[83] Many law enforcement agencies in developed democracies have adopted such interviewing protocols, similar to what has been recommended for law enforcement personnel by the U.S. National Institute of Justice.[84] Evidence based forensic interviewing techniques involve the use of a particular way of interviewing witnesses and victims of violence, by highly trained personnel. Such techniques are commonly used in situations where witness trauma and vulnerability may influence the nature of disclosures. The goal of using such techniques is to increase the prevalence of uncovering the truth while minimizing the re-traumatization of witnesses and victims.[85] Evidence based forensic interviewing include techniques such as establishing rapport with the witness, avoiding leading questions (by 'putting words into a witness' mouth'), using open-ended questions, and also includes training on evaluation of testimony credibility and confirming the data through alternate sources.[86] Scholars and UN observers note the importance of fact-finding investigators being trained in forensic interviewing techniques in order to improve witness evidence, but note that without standardized methodological standards guiding this process, there is no guarantee that such techniques will be adopted as authoritative on a uniform basis.

---

[82] Robertson, "Human Rights and Fact Finding", 42.
[83] Also referred to as forensic interview techniques, or the 'cognitive interview'.
[84] Office of Justice: National Institute of Justice (NIJ). "Eyewitness Testimony: A Guide for Law Enforcement (1999) http://www.nij.gov/pubs-sum/178240.htm.
[85] Ibid.
[86] Ibid.

The Role of NGOs and Members of Civil Society

The results of this study revealed that the nature of the relationship between the UN and NGOs, such as human rights organizations, as well as other members of civil society (i.e., independent journalists, media outlets, etc.) was rarely transparent. In those reports that did reference collaboration with NGOs, serious questions could be raised regarding the political agendas of the NGOs, and human rights advocates with regard to potential bias and alliances. No report included explicit information on whether information was received or shared with any media outlet, thus this dynamic could not be effectively evaluated. NGOs and journalists reporting on human rights abuses play a key role in the investigation of international human rights violations. The protection of NGO personnel, such as human rights advocates, and journalists (as well as their sources) is vital to the success of many fact-finding missions. While there has been some controversy regarding the extent to which human rights advocates' working with NGOs and journalists' sources can be afforded the privilege of confidentiality, Robertson notes how consistently court decisions have supported NGO and journalist requests to keep their sources confidential, deeming it to be in the public's best interest to do so, as well as in the best interest of human rights reporters and their sources who would likely be placed at great risk if their identities were disclosed.[87]

NGOs and journalists reporting on human rights abuses can also contribute to bias (or at least the appearance of bias), particularly since a significant number of witness statements used in international fact-finding missions emanate from NGO human rights reporters working in conflict zones. Concerns about the role NGOs and journalists play in international fact-finding missions relate to making their relationship with the UN transparent, as well as substantiating the methodology these entities use in obtaining witness testimony. Robertson recommends caution regarding those members of the international human rights community who have a "propaganda agenda or report on wars where they support one side or the other," and then produce biased evidence that is relied upon by international fact-finding mission personnel.[88] Bassiouni refers to the often inter-dependent relationship between the UN and the NGO human rights community as "incestuous", noting that at times powerful NGOs pressure the UN for particular outcomes, which has the potential of influencing various aspects of the investigative process.

---

[87] Ibid.
[88] Ibid., 18.

In fact, the watchdog organization, NGO Monitor recently filed a submission with the HRC expressing concern over the a recent HRC fact-finding mission on Israel, in regard to the influential role the NGO human rights community has on UN fact-finding missions. The submission cited the UN's increasing reliance on NGOs for 'on the ground' information about alleged human rights violations, and the veiled nature of this relationship. The complaint referenced a previous incident involving a well-known and highly influential human rights organization that provided information to UN fact-finding investigators that was included in the final report only to be later removed when it was determined that the information was incorrect. The complaint noted the lack of any methodological standards used in UN fact-finding missions to verify the veracity of NGO allegations, which they noted not only resulted in significant harm to the country of Israel, but also compromised the credibility of the entire fact-finding mission.

NGO Monitor's submission demanded at a minimum that the UN Mission to Israel strictly adhere to the principles of "universality, impartiality, objectivity and non-selectivity, constructive international dialogue and cooperation, transparency...in all interactions with NGOs."[89] Further, it demanded that the Commission develop and adhere to "professional guidelines for assessing the credibility and factual and legal claims of NGOs," particularly in light of the fact that many human rights organizations now have budgets and influence that "rival that of large multinational corporations, such as Amnesty International, Human Rights Watch, and Oxfam."[90] NGO Monitor's submission stressed the need for the UN to "at a minimum...identify all individuals involved in its work, adopt transparency standards governing all interactions with NGOs, and implement guidelines as to how the credibility and factual claims of NGOs will be assessed."[91]

NGO Monitor's submission reflects the growing recognition of the interdependent relationship between the UN and the NGO community, and the need for increased transparency in the nature of this relationship. The role of NGOs, including human rights organizations is vitally important to the success of international fact-finding missions, particularly with regard to their ability to obtain evidence 'on the ground,' yet increased transparency

---

[89] "NGO Monitor Submission to the UN Human Rights Council Independent International Fact-finding Mission on the Israeli Settlements in the Occupied Palestinian Territory including East Jerusalem Pursuant to HRC Resolution 19/7," NGO Monitor, (October 30, 2012): 22, accessed January 16, 2013 http://www.ngo-monitor.org/data/images/File/NGO_Monitor-Submission_to_the_Settlements_Fact_Finding_Committee.pdf.
[90] Ibid., 2.
[91] Ibid., 22.

regarding how NGOs obtained evidence proffered to the commissioners will enable the commissioners to effectively vet the evidence obtained from NGOs. Additionally, the issue of transparency in the hiring of commissioners and mission personnel, with prior (or current) associations with NGOs and media outlets, particularly if such organizations have biased agendas, and predetermined perspectives on conflicts involving alleged human rights abuses. While it may be an impossible task to hire commissioners with expertise who have not developed opinions on the dynamics of a situation, an effective vetting process can ascertain a commissioner's ability to render objective assessments despite personal bias.

Budgets and Resource Allocation

Evaluating how fact-finding missions are financed and how financial resources are allocated and managed was virtually impossible, based upon the information contained in all. The exception to this was the Bahrain Commission report which included comprehensive budget information, made available on a public website. Appropriate financial support for factfinding missions in large part reflects the commitment of the sponsor to the mission's successful implementation and facilitation. A poorly funded mission will likely result in a poorly staffed mission of short duration. Thus, despite the commonly held assertion that "financing commissions of inquiry by the regular UN budget is a guarantee of their impartiality,"[92] resource allocation is often politically motivated in accordance with the priorities of UN Member States.[93] The disparity in funding of fact-finding missions affects every aspect of the inquiry process, including the staffing of missions, time in the region, duration of the mission. Poorly funded factfinding missions also negatively impact the ability of missions to sufficiently protect witnesses, victims and detainees, since poorly funded missions do not have the resources to sufficiently protect witnesses and their families, particularly once the mission has been completed.[94]

---

[92] Geneva Academy of International Humanitarian Law, "The UN Human Rights Council", 2.
[93] Bassiouni, "Appraising UN-justice".
[94] Boutruche, "Credible Fact-Finding", 119.

Implications for Best Practice in Fact-finding Missions

This study yielded valuable information that can be utilized in the development of a universal and standardized methodology that can be applied to international and national fact-finding missions, reflecting best practice principles. Any standardized framework must be comprehensive enough to be applied universally, but flexible enough to be adapted to unique mission circumstances.

Mandates

Mandates should be unbiased, reflecting neutrality and impartiality. Mission boundaries and parameters should be clear, with the establishment of clear objectives that can easily be interpreted. Final reports should include a comprehensive summary of all substantive issues that were debated regarding the wording of the mandate. Interpretations of the mandate should be clear and explicit. Both the original mandate and the interpretation should be included in the final fact-finding report.

Appointment of Commissioners and Hiring of Mission Personnel

Titles of mission members should be standardized among all fact-finding missions, with each role having a designated title that is descriptive. Information on how Commissioners, staff, and experts are selected and vetted for conflict of interest must be included in the final report. The process for selecting commissioners, experts and investigators (as well as all other personnel in decision-making positions) should be explicit and included in the final report. Vetting of commissioners should include ideological positions whenever possible, that may influence independence and impartiality, or give the appearance of compromising impartiality and objectivity.

Mission candidates must be made public as early as possible in the selection process, with all relevant parties, including UN Member States, and subject nation States, having 30 days to respond with any objections. If mission personnel, including Commissioners have objections lodged against them, the mandating agency must respond to parties lodging complaints, providing a comprehensive rationale if a decision is made to appoint a particular Commissioner (or other key personnel member) despite objections.

Comprehensive information about commissioners must be included in appended CVs that conform to a particular format. CVs should include all educational and professional credentials, professional employment positions including experience in international humanitarian and human rights organizations, NGOs, government positions, including past military service, volunteer service, international travel, knowledge of the country involved, all publications (peer-reviewed and lay), social media accounts, languages spoken, and nationality. Similar information should be included on all members of mission personnel, particularly those in decision-making capacities.

All commissioners and mission personnel in decision-making capacities must sign an ethical Code of Conduct, and Terms of Agreement outlining their roles, functions, and responsibilities. Mission Commissioners must reflect gender, ethnic and geographical diversity to the greatest extent possible. Each mission must also include a master's level social worker, for consultative and advocacy purposes in relation to witnesses and victims associated with the investigation. All commission personnel should undergo training focusing on cultural competence, language, data collection and analysis techniques, management of witnesses, victims and detainees, including formal training on forensic interviewing techniques, as well as the nature of trauma. Training should also include information on evidence management, including various standards of proof, and the collection and preservation of evidence. The nature and duration of this training should be included in the final report.

Terms of Reference

Mission Commissioners should draft comprehensive Terms of Reference early in the investigative process. Terms of Reference should include detailed objectives for the mission with an associated timeline, with criteria for how objectives will be met. A list of required resources (human and physical) will be prepared with an associated detailed budget, with the assistance of an approved accounting firm. Prior to the mission being initiated the Commissioners must be able to illustrate that the mandate objectives, goals and associated activities can be sufficiently supported by the budget. The Terms of Reference will also stipulate the methodology to be used during the investigation.

Investigative Methodology and Report Compilation

The methodology used in the mission must be transparent and support the principles of independence and impartiality. The evidence and standard of proof must be stated explicitly and conform to standards of credibility accepted in broader disciplines, including the social sciences, biological (or "hard") sciences, and/or criminal justice fields. The methods section should make clear the chain of custody of all evidence, and how the evidence fits within the scope of the mission objectives (to ensure that the mission remains within the intended scope as prescribed by the mandate). The origin of evidence must be made explicit and include the chain of custody of the evidence and how it was secured throughout the investigation. The report should explain in detail how each piece of evidence was gathered and how fact-checking was completed. At the very least, the identities of sources should be recorded and kept securely by the Commission and acknowledgement made of possible conflicts of interest, and vetting of information. The mission report should reference what type of software and/or database was used to secure the evidence of facts. Methods used for recording direct observations and perceptions must be included in the report as well.

At a minimum, all reports should include the date the UN resolution was passed initiating the fact-finding mission, the commissioners appointed, the date that commissioners began working on the mission, the beginning and ending date of the mission, and fieldwork in the country, dates and subject of all follow-up meetings after completion of fieldwork, date the report was finalized and submitted to the mandating agency. A section on relevant socio-political/cultural history of the regions and all sub-groups involved, including comprehensive history of religious and/or ethnic conflict should be included in the report. All statements of fact in this regard should be supported by scholarly sources. Mission duration must be explicit with a rationale that connects the mandate, budget (resources), and mission objectives to ensure that the objectives of the mission can be sufficiently met. Reports should include explicit information regarding previous and/or simultaneous investigations into the same incidents, since duplicative efforts may impact the quality of evidence, as well as potentially re-traumatizing witnesses and victims.

Recommendations Regarding Witnesses and Victims

Testimony from witnesses and victims should be clearly documented, including how the information was obtained. The report should make clear whether testimony from witnesses and victims is direct, or from a secondary source, such as an NGO. The report should make clear whether testimony from witnesses and victims involve first-hand information or hearsay. All witnesses, victims and detainees should be provided with informed consent and information on the limits of confidentiality, prior to consenting to be interviewed. The UN should create a confidentiality policy similar to that used by psychologists and social workers, which articulates the obligations of the mandating agency/organization to keep identifying information confidential. Civil and/or criminal liability should be built into such an agreement in response to anyone who knowingly violates confidentiality. All staff (including interpreters) who are in contact with victims and witnesses should undergo sufficient training in working with trauma survivors. Prior to interviews the interviewees should be asked about their concerns and needs, as well as whether they have previously offered their testimony to any other party, including UN personnel, international aid workers, NGO personnel, or journalists.

All witnesses, victims and advocates should be asked if they desire an advocate to be present with them during any interviews. Identifying information of all interviewees shall be documented, including demographic information, as well as reported ethnonational, religious and political alliances (whenever possible), and kept confidential by the mission in a manner that complies with best practice. Forensic interviewing techniques should be utilized conforming to best practice. A list of the interview questions should be prepared in advance of all interviews whenever possible and should conform to best practice, avoiding leading questions, bias, and threatening, or encouraging tone. Such a list should not limit the interviewers ability to deviate from initially planned questions, since often in investigations, interviewers must remain flexible and adapt to interviewee responses, but they should serve as guides. A list of interview questions should be appended to the final report.

A description of the interviews conducted should be included in the final report, including whether witnesses were interviewed individually, or in groups, alone, or with an advocate. All witnesses, victims and detainees should undergo a thorough vetting process for conflicts of interest prior to a determination of the level of credibility. A database system should be utilized that would signal possible duplicity of witnesses and statements. All witness statements should be typed and signed by all parties involved in the interview, including interpreters. All witness statements (oral and written) should be supported by corroborating evidence whenever possible, including additional eyewitness testimony, physical evidence such as medical evidence, cultural and text artifacts.

Witnesses, victims and detainees should receive full disclosure of the limits of protection the mission can offer, including whether such protection will extend beyond the timeframe of the mission, who will be offered protection (i.e., individual, family, extended family members), and what the protection consists of (i.e., psychological, physical, and the level of security). A protection plan should be put into place prior to interviews being conducted. If commissioners determine that the safety concerns of witnesses, victims and detainees can not be sufficiently met in the short and long term, then a decision must be made as to whether the interviews should be conducted, and a comprehensive rationale in that regard should be included in the final report as to the decision made.

Collaboration between the mandating agency and NGOs, governments, other UN agencies, and civil society, including media outlets and independent journalists should be made explicit, including what information and evidence is proffered to the mandating agency, and how the information and evidence was obtained and vetted. The nature of relationships between the fact-finding mandating agency and the NGOs, governments, other UN agencies, and civil society, including media outlets and independent journalists should be made explicit, particularly with regard to the exchange of information and personnel. The nature of such relationships should be regulated and transparent. Evidence provided by NGOs and other humanitarian organizations that cannot be verified in the same manner as evidence directly obtained by the mission, should be disregarded. All names of collaborating NGOs, media outlets and journalists, government officials, and members of civil society should be included in the final report.

Recommendations Regarding Budgets and Resource Allocation

A detailed budget should be made available, either appended to the final report, or posted on a public website. The budget must be detailed enough to indicate resource allocation decisions, including salaries and other related expenditures. The budget must reflect that the mission is funded at a level that supports the mandate objectives. The budget should be audited regularly throughout the mission, with the budget, and final audit being posted on a pubic website, or appended to the final report.

LIMITATIONS OF THE STUDY

Despite the vast amount of data yielded from this study, there were limitations, many of which were related to challenges in operationalizing variables that had not been previously defined by the UN, or within the literature. Thus, the process of defining variables within this study, while based upon the literature whenever possible, was at times subjective. For instance, few reports were explicit in terms of the duration of the mission, thus duration was often determined based upon subjective indicators, such as an initial meeting of Commissioners, and the submission of a final report. Calculations of number of staff, for instance, were also at times subjective. For instance, since virtually no report stated definitively and clearly the number staff hired, reviewers had to interpret this information from various sections of a report that made generalized references to various staff working in various contexts. Thus while every effort was made to accurately assess whether a report referenced the number of staff hired, often conclusions were based upon liberal interpretations of references to staff strewn throughout a given report. Another example of the subjectivity involved in assessing variables relates to whether investigators were allowed access to physical sites. Very few reports provided explicit information in this regard, but rather made references throughout the report to various physical sites having been inspected, thus reviewers rated this variable liberally based upon their subjective interpretations. In other words, a considerable amount of subjective interpretation was exercised in the quantitative evaluation of variables, which is reflective of the ambiguous way in which most foundational information about the missions was included throughout the majority of the reports evaluated.

Other limitations related to the difficulty in locating COI reports online, as there does not appear to be much consistency exercised in where such reports are posted, particularly older reports. Another limitation related to the decision to limit the data collection to information contained only within the reports. The goal of this study was specifically to compare the information contained across reports, thus preventing the inclusion of data that may have been helpful to the broader understanding of how commissions of inquiry go about their investigations and report writing. For example, we could have obtained additional budget information in order to assess how differences in budgets may have impacted the length of an investigation. However, this was beyond the scope of this particular study. Future studies may focus on correlations between these variables and call for the inclusion of multiple sources of data to fill in missing information regarding variables impacting the investigations.

Additional future studies that may build from the results of this study include the empirical evaluation of other types of fact-finding missions, such as Special Procedures, and Group of Expert reports. Comparisons of various types of fact-finding missions may also yield valuable information and contribute ultimately to the development of best practice principles, the adoption of such principles, and their general and specific efficacy when utilized by fact-finding missions.

Appendices to the Empirical Analysis of United Nations Commissions of Inquiry

Appendix 1

Reports Evaluated in Sample

Report Citation	Report Title	Report Date	Subject State/Interest (referred to as)
A/33/331	Study of Reported Violations of human rights in Chile, with particular reference to torture and other cruel, inhuman or degrading treatment or punishment	10/25/1978	Chile Commission
A/59/370	Report of the independent expert of the Commission on Human Rights on the situation of human rights in Afghanistan	9/21/2004	Afghanistan Commission
A/9621	Report of the Commission of Inquiry on the Reported Massacres in Mozambique	5/27/1905	Mozambique Commission
A/HRC/12/48	Report of the United Nations Fact Finding Mission on the Gaza Conflict	9/25/2009	Gaza Conflict Commission
A/HRC/13/66	Report of the United Nations High Commission for Human Rights on the violation of human rights in Honduras since the coup d'état on 28 June 2009	3/10/2010	Honduras Commission

Siracusa Guidelines for International, Regional and
National Fact-finding Bodies

Report Citation	Report Title	Report Date	Subject State/Interest (referred to as)
A/HRC/15/21	Report of the international fact-finding mission to investigate violations of international law, including international humanitarian and human rights law, resulting from the Israeli attacks on the flotilla of ships carrying humanitarian assistance	9/27/2010	Flotilla Incident Commission
A/HRC/15/50	Report of the Committee of Independent Experts in international humanitarian and human rights laws to monitor and assess any domestic, legal or other proceedings undertaken by both the Government of Israel and the Palestinian side, in light of General Assembly resolution 64/254, including the independence, effectiveness, genuineness of these investigations and their conformity with international standards	9/23/2010	Israel/Palestinian Territories Commission
A/HRC/17/49	Report of the United Nations High Commissioner for Human Rights on the situation of human rights in Côte d'Ivoire	6/14/2011	Côte d'Ivoire Commission
A/HRC/18/21	Report of the High Commissioner on OHCHR's visit to Yemen	9/13/2011	Yemen Commission
A/HRC/18/53	Report of the United Nations High Commissioner for Human Rights on the situation of human rights in the Syrian Arab Republic	9/15/2011	Syria Commission
A/HRC/19/68	Report of the International Commission of Inquiry on Libya	3/8/2012	Libya Commission
A/HRC/3/2	Report of the Commission of Inquiry on Lebanon pursuant to Human Rights Council resolution S-2/1	11/23/2006	Lebanon Commission

Appendix 1

Report Citation	Report Title	Report Date	Subject State/Interest (referred to as)
A/HRC/4/80	Report of the High-level Mission on the situation of human rights in Darfur pursuant to Human Rights Council decision S-4/101	3/9/2007	2007 Darfur Commission
A/HRC/9/26	Report of the high-level fact-finding mission to Beit Hanoun established under Council resolution S-3/1	9/1/2008	Beit Hanoun Commission
CH-1211 GENEVE 10	Report from OHCHR Fact-Finding mission to Kenya, 6–28 February 2008	2/28/2008	Kenya Commission
E/CN.4/1995/23	Violations of Human Rights in Southern Africa: Report of the Ad Hoc Working Group of Experts	1/13/1995	South Africa Commission
E/CN.4/2001/134	Report of the International Commission of Inquiry for Togo	2/22/2001	Togo Commission
E/CN.4/2006/119	Report of the Mission to Kyrgyzstan by the Office of the High Commissioner of Human Rights concerning the Killings in Andijan, Uzbekistan of 13–14 May 2005	7/12/2005	Uzbekistan Commission
None	Report of the OHCHR Mission to Egypt 27 March to 4 April 2011		Egypt Commission
None	Report of the OHCHR Assessment Mission to Tunisia 26 January to 2 February 2011		Tunisia Commission
S/1994/674	Final Report of the Commission of Experts [for former Yugoslavia] Established Pursuant to Security Council Resolution 780 (1992)	5/27/1994	Yugoslavia Commission
S/1999/1257	Report of the Independent Inquiry into the actions of the United Nations during the 1994 Genocide in Rwanda	12/16/1999	Rwanda Commission
S/RES/1049	International Commission of Inquiry established under resolution 1012 (1995) concerning Burundi	3/5/1996	Burundi Commission

Intersentia

Report Citation	Report Title	Report Date	Subject State/Interest (referred to as)
	Bahrain Independent Commission of Inquiry	12/10/2011	Bahrain Commission
None	Report of the International Commission of Inquiry on Darfur to the United Nations Secretary General Pursuant to Security Council Resolution 1564 of 18 September 2004	1/25/2005	2005 Darfur Commission
S/2009/693	Report of the International Commission of Inquiry mandated to establish the facts and circumstances of the events of 28 September 2009 in Guinea	12/18/2009	Guinea Commission
A/5630	Report of the United Nations Fact-Finding Mission to South Vietnam	12/7/1963	South Vietnam Commission
	Report of the Group of Experts for Cambodia established pursuant to General Assembly resolution 52/135		Cambodia Commission
S/2005/203	International Independent Investigation Commission regarding the assassination of the former President of Lebanon, Rafiq Hariri	3/25/2005	Lebanon Commission
A/HRC/10/59	Combined report of seven thematic special procedures on technical assistance to the Government of the Democratic Republic of the Congo and urgent examination of the situation in the east of the country	3/5/2009	DRC Commission

Appendix 2

Quantitative Variables

What was the duration of investigation?
What was the total number of pages in the report?
Was a summary of the facts included?
Summary of facts alleged:
Was a list of the human rights violations that were involved included?
Was submission of the evidence documented?
Were the facts established?
Were conclusions reached?
Did the State consent to the COI?
Did the State and the UN enter into an agreed terms of engagement?
Was there a prior or simultaneous investigation into the same incident(s)?
Was there any follow-up investigation mandated?
Was the methodology explicitly described?
What was the total number of commissioners assigned to the investigation?
Were the names of the commissioners included in the report?
Did the commissioners sign a code of conduct?
What was the total number of staff assigned to the investigation?
Were the names of the staff members included in the report?
Did the staff members sign a code of conduct?
What was the total number of experts assigned to the investigation?
Were the names of the experts included in the report?
Did the experts sign a code of conduct?
Was a conflict of interest checks completed on the commissioners?
Was a conflict of interest checks completed on the experts?
Was a conflict of interest checks completed on the witnesses?
Were the investigators allowed access to witnesses?
Were the investigators allowed access to detainees?
Were the investigators allowed access to all sites?
Were the witnesses interviewed privately?
Were the witnesses offered protection?

What was the number of witnesses interviewed?
Was witness/victim interview methodology explicit?
Was the amount of the budget included in the report?
Was the budget disclosed to the public?
Was the budget audited?
Was the audit published?

Appendix 3

Operationalization of Quantitative Variables

COI Report Date: The date of publication, not the date of the commission

Subject State/Interest: Included in the Title

Mandate: Include this in quotations. Be comprehensive. Note whether the mandate interpretation is explicit and whether the entire mandate was included (from the Resolution).

Duration of Investigation: Either stated explicitly in the report, or calculated based on dates given. This refers to the duration from the beginning of the commission to the submission of the report, and not solely the time in the country. If there is a delay between the passing of the resolution and drafting of the mandate to the initiation of the first meeting of the commissioners, the date used will be the first time that the commissioners met as a team. The end date is when the report is published.

Methodology Stated Explicitly: Does the report describe in detail how the investigation occurred with regard to standards for proof of evidence, chain of custody, framework used in all aspects of the investigation. What kind of experts with what training? Who was in the country and who was not? Could someone repeat the investigation using this report as a roadmap for exactly how the investigation was carried out?

State Consent to COI: The level of subject state cooperation/consent

State/UN Terms of Engagement: Did the country and the UN come to some agreement on how the COI was to be carried out?

Interview Methodology Explicit: Did the report reference how witnesses were interviewed? Were there any evidence-based interviewing techniques used? Were interviewed conducted by commissioners? Staff? NGOs? Were counselors or advocates present? Did they occur in person or in writing?

Appendix 4
Thematic Guiding Questions for Qualitative Review

Theme 1 – Commissioners, Experts, Staff

Identifying and Background Information for Investigative Personnel
- Were the names of all commissioners, interpreters, investigators, experts and staff included?
- Were the CVs of commissioners, interpreters, investigators and experts appended to the report?
- Did the report include all credentials, including experience in international humanitarian and human rights NGOs, and knowledge of the country involved?
- Did the report include information on conflict of interest checks? If so, how thorough were these?
- Did any vetting include ideological positions of all investigative personnel?
- Did any vetting include past government positions? UN? NGOs?

Selection Requirements/Procedures for Hiring Personnel
- Did the report state how the commissioners, experts and staff were selected?
- Did the report state who selected the Commissioners? The Experts? The Staff?
- Did the report note why commissioners/experts were deemed qualified for the particular position?
- Did the report note whether any subject government(s) objected to the appointment of any member of the commission, and why?
- Did the report include the criteria used to appoint the staff to their position?

- Any scholarly publications that indicate the expertise of commissioners, either in the region, or in the area of human rights?
- Was there opposition to the selection of any of the commissioners? If so, from whom, and for what reasons?
- Who went to the country? Does the report state whether the entire team visited the country, or just select staff members?

Training of Personnel
- Does the report indicate whether there was any training upon arrival to the country? If so what does the training consist of and in what format?
- Did the commissioners and staff undergo any training/preparation that included understanding the historical/social/cultural/political dynamics of the country/conflict?
- Are commissioners and staff trained regarding various standards of proof, and how to collect and preserve evidence? Chain of custody considerations, language training, interviewing techniques, and managing witnesses and victims of trauma?
- Did the report reference whether commissioners or staff spoke the language of the subject country, and/or the native language of all witnesses? Did they use translators? What methodology was used for translations/interpreters?

Theme 2 – COI Construction

Initial Formation of COI
- Does the report indicate the timeframe for commissioners to assemble a team for a mission?
- Does the report indicate clearly the objectives of the Mission?
- What, if any, substantive issues were debated regarding the need for a COI?
- Was the process of the initial development and planning of the COI transparent? If so, how? What process ensued, over what timeframe?

Duration
- Does the report indicate how the allotted timeframe for a particular mission was determined?
- Does the report indicate the criteria used for determining the time allotted in the country? Were safety issues and/or budget limitations referenced?

Mandate Wording

- Does the report include the exact wording of the mandate included in the Resolution? (for UN COIs).
- Does the report reference whether any substantive issues were debated regarding the wording of the mandate?
- Did the report include whether there was a minority position regarding the wording of the mandate
- Does the mandate appear balanced?
- Did the commissioners note any concerns about the wording of the mandate?
- Did the report include the commissioners' interpretation of the mandate? Was the process for interpretation made explicit? How?
- Where there any differences between the official mandate and what was actually carried out in the mission? If so, what were these differences?

Theme 3 – Witnesses, Victims, Detainees

Selection
- Was the vetting of witnesses made clear and involve a process that is standardized and accepted in the field of inquiry? (*beyond UN, NGO).
- Was there any attempt to conduct a conflict of interest check on witnesses?
- Was there any attempt to triangulate eye-witness testimony with alternate sources of information?
- Did the report reference whether witness testimony was first-hand, second-hand, hearsay? Did the report state explicitly who did the interviewing? NGOs? Commissioners? Staff?
- Was contextual/demographic information obtained on witnesses?
- Was informed consent provided?
- Did the report state how the Mission contacted witnesses and other persons of interest?

Protection
- What is the mission doing to protect the civilians that are reporting personal violations? Is this information contained in the report in any type of substantive manner?
- How did they protect witnesses/victims?
- How can the mission ensure that the victims are protected under the government of the state? How long is protection offered? Solely during the time of the mission, or after?

- Was identifying information collected on witnesses, and if not, then how was protection offered?
- Were witnesses asked specifically what they feared and what they needed?

Interviewing
- Did victims have social workers/advocates with them during the interview?
- Was a list of interview questions appended to the report?
- Did the report reference how witnesses were interviewed?
- What techniques were used? Were the techniques forensic and evidence-based?
- Did the report reference how information about the interviews (transcripts) was held? Electronically? Hand-written notes?
- Were the questions administered neutrality?
- Were questions leading? Biased? Intimidating? Threatening to victims?
- Under what conditions were subjects interviewed? Open space? Private room?
- Majority of reports failed to give any methodology on interviewing techniques,
- Were steps taken to ensure that witnesses were not interviewed more than once?
- Did the report indicate whether all witness testimony occurred in person, or were some submitted in writing?
- Were interviews confidential?
- Did the report indicate who was in the room during face-to-face interviews? Were interviews conducted in group format, or individually?
- Did the report indicate whether witnesses who came forward were also included in testimony proffered by NGOs?

Theme 4 – Standardization
- Report Organization – Was there an attempt to organize the COI reports in a particular manner?
- Did the report include socio-political/historical context that is cited with scholarly sources?
- Did the report include a comprehensive Methods section? If so, what did it include? Could the investigation be replicated? Are the conclusions falsifiable?
- Was a map of the country/region included, with notations of conflict zones?

Appendix 4

- Does the report its length? (Why are some reports 30 pages and some 500?)
- Did the report include comprehensive information about the budget? And allocation of funds?
- Does the report state how the subject government(s) responded to the COI?
- Does the report reference state and non-state actor involvement/agendas?
- Are there multinational corporations exerting major influence on one faction or another?
- Is the mission using neutral language to write the report, if not, how can the reports reflect neutrality so all sides can cooperate?

Methodology
- Does the report include any reference to a particular methodology used? Is this information sufficiently detailed?
- What methods are being used for security of information obtained?
- Did the report/commissioners rely on scholarly sources when appropriate? Are all statements of facts being supported by reliable sources?
- Do methods used conform to current research practices, such as the Scientific Method – quantitative and qualitative methodology, and/or criminal investigation standards established in the field?
- What method does the commission use to record direct observations and perceptions?
- Who writes which sections of the final report? Who is the author? What guidelines do they have/use?
- What is the scope of collaboration for the final report?

Theme 5 – Evidence

Reliability
- Did the report include any reference to the standard level of proof required for evidence, chain of custody, management and expert evaluations?
- How credible/reliable are the reports?
- Was there triangulation of the data whenever possible?
- Does the report describe in detail how each piece of evidence was gathered and how fact-checking was completed?
- Does the standard of proof used comply with the mandate?

- Was there a clear attempt to obtain evidence from all sides of the conflict in order to avoid bias?
- Did the report include detailed information about sites visited, including what sites were visited, at what time, who inspected the site and what evidence/information was obtained?
- Did the report address the source of all evidence and information?
   - Did the report state whether evidence was obtained directly by mission personnel, or was obtained from NGOs, government ministers, media, or other members of civil society?
- If the report references information and evidence obtained from a third party, was information included on how the source and information/evidence was vetted for conflict of interest?

Theme 6 – Outcomes

Conclusions and Recommendations
- How is data analyzed for conclusions (*what standards exist*)?
- How are conclusions/recommendations drawn? Was the report explicit about this process?
- Did the report address victim compensation/reparations and perpetrator accountability?
- Did the report reference follow-up steps recommendations?

UN Documents

United Nations   A/RES/67/1

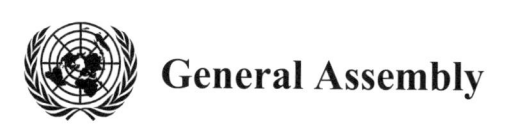

General Assembly

Distr.: General
30 November 2012

Sixty-seventh session
Agenda item 83

Resolution adopted by the General Assembly

[*without reference to a Main Committee (A/67/L.1)*]

67/1. Declaration of the High-level Meeting of the General Assembly on the Rule of Law at the National and International Levels

The General Assembly

Adopts the following Declaration:

Declaration of the High-level Meeting of the General Assembly on the Rule of Law at the National and International Levels

We, Heads of State and Government, and heads of delegation have gathered at United Nations Headquarters in New York on 24 September 2012 to reaffirm our commitment to the rule of law and its fundamental importance for political dialogue and cooperation among all States and for the further development of the three main pillars upon which the United Nations is built: international peace and security, human rights and development. We agree that our collective response to the challenges and opportunities arising from the many complex political, social and economic transformations before us must be guided by the rule of law, as it is the foundation of friendly and equitable relations between States and the basis on which just and fair societies are built.

I

1. We reaffirm our solemn commitment to the purposes and principles of the Charter of the United Nations, international law and justice, and to an international order based on the rule of law, which are indispensable foundations for a more peaceful, prosperous and just world.

2. We recognize that the rule of law applies to all States equally, and to international organizations, including the United Nations and its principal organs, and that respect for and promotion of the rule of law and justice should guide all of their activities and accord predictability and legitimacy to their actions. We also recognize that all persons, institutions and entities, public and private, including the State itself, are accountable to just, fair and equitable laws and are entitled without any discrimination to equal protection of the law.

Please recycle

3. We are determined to establish a just and lasting peace all over the world, in accordance with the purposes and principles of the Charter of the United Nations. We rededicate ourselves to support all efforts to uphold the sovereign equality of all States, to respect their territorial integrity and political independence, to refrain in our international relations from the threat or use of force in any manner inconsistent with the purposes and principles of the United Nations, and to uphold the resolution of disputes by peaceful means and in conformity with the principles of justice and international law, the right to self-determination of peoples which remain under colonial domination and foreign occupation, non-interference in the internal affairs of States, respect for human rights and fundamental freedoms, respect for the equal rights of all without distinction as to race, sex, language or religion, international cooperation in solving international problems of an economic, social, cultural or humanitarian character, and the fulfilment in good faith of the obligations assumed in accordance with the Charter.

4. We reaffirm the duty of all States to settle their international disputes by peaceful means, inter alia through negotiation, enquiry, good offices, mediation, conciliation, arbitration and judicial settlement, or other peaceful means of their own choice.

5. We reaffirm that human rights, the rule of law and democracy are interlinked and mutually reinforcing and that they belong to the universal and indivisible core values and principles of the United Nations.

6. We reaffirm the solemn commitment of our States to fulfil their obligations to promote universal respect for, and the observance and protection of, all human rights and fundamental freedoms for all. The universal nature of these rights and freedoms is beyond question. We emphasize the responsibilities of all States, in conformity with the Charter of the United Nations, to respect human rights and fundamental freedoms for all, without distinction of any kind.

7. We are convinced that the rule of law and development are strongly interrelated and mutually reinforcing, that the advancement of the rule of law at the national and international levels is essential for sustained and inclusive economic growth, sustainable development, the eradication of poverty and hunger and the full realization of all human rights and fundamental freedoms, including the right to development, all of which in turn reinforce the rule of law, and for this reason we are convinced that this interrelationship should be considered in the post-2015 international development agenda.

8. We recognize the importance of fair, stable and predictable legal frameworks for generating inclusive, sustainable and equitable development, economic growth and employment, generating investment and facilitating entrepreneurship, and in this regard we commend the work of the United Nations Commission on International Trade Law in modernizing and harmonizing international trade law.

9. States are strongly urged to refrain from promulgating and applying any unilateral economic, financial or trade measures not in accordance with international law and the Charter of the United Nations that impede the full achievement of economic and social development, particularly in developing countries.

10. We recognize the progress made by countries in advancing the rule of law as an integral part of their national strategies. We also recognize that there are common features founded on international norms and standards which are reflected in a broad diversity of national experiences in the area of the rule of law. In this regard, we

stress the importance of promoting the sharing of national practices and of inclusive dialogue.

11. We recognize the importance of national ownership in rule of law activities, strengthening justice and security institutions that are accessible and responsive to the needs and rights of all individuals and which build trust and promote social cohesion and economic prosperity.

12. We reaffirm the principle of good governance and commit to an effective, just, non-discriminatory and equitable delivery of public services pertaining to the rule of law, including criminal, civil and administrative justice, commercial dispute settlement and legal aid.

13. We are convinced that the independence of the judicial system, together with its impartiality and integrity, is an essential prerequisite for upholding the rule of law and ensuring that there is no discrimination in the administration of justice.

14. We emphasize the right of equal access to justice for all, including members of vulnerable groups, and the importance of awareness-raising concerning legal rights, and in this regard we commit to taking all necessary steps to provide fair, transparent, effective, non-discriminatory and accountable services that promote access to justice for all, including legal aid.

15. We acknowledge that informal justice mechanisms, when in accordance with international human rights law, play a positive role in dispute resolution, and that everyone, particularly women and those belonging to vulnerable groups, should enjoy full and equal access to these justice mechanisms.

16. We recognize the importance of ensuring that women, on the basis of the equality of men and women, fully enjoy the benefits of the rule of law, and commit to using law to uphold their equal rights and ensure their full and equal participation, including in institutions of governance and the judicial system, and recommit to establishing appropriate legal and legislative frameworks to prevent and address all forms of discrimination and violence against women and to secure their empowerment and full access to justice.

17. We recognize the importance of the rule of law for the protection of the rights of the child, including legal protection from discrimination, violence, abuse and exploitation, ensuring the best interests of the child in all actions, and recommit to the full implementation of the rights of the child.

18. We emphasize the importance of the rule of law as one of the key elements of conflict prevention, peacekeeping, conflict resolution and peacebuilding, stress that justice, including transitional justice, is a fundamental building block of sustainable peace in countries in conflict and post-conflict situations, and stress the need for the international community, including the United Nations, to assist and support such countries, upon their request, as they may face special challenges during their transition.

19. We stress the importance of supporting national civilian capacity development and institution-building in the aftermath of conflict, including through peacekeeping operations in accordance with their mandates, with a view to delivering more effective civilian capacities, as well as enhanced, international, regional, North-South, South-South and triangular cooperation, including in the field of the rule of law.

20. We stress that greater compliance with international humanitarian law is an indispensable prerequisite for improving the situation of victims of armed conflict,

and we reaffirm the obligation of all States and all parties to armed conflict to respect and ensure respect for international humanitarian law in all circumstances, and also stress the need for wide dissemination and full implementation of international humanitarian law at the national level.

21. We stress the importance of a comprehensive approach to transitional justice incorporating the full range of judicial and non-judicial measures to ensure accountability, serve justice, provide remedies to victims, promote healing and reconciliation, establish independent oversight of the security system and restore confidence in the institutions of the State and promote the rule of law. In this respect, we underline that truth-seeking processes, including those that investigate patterns of past violations of international human rights law and international humanitarian law and their causes and consequences, are important tools that can complement judicial processes.

22. We commit to ensuring that impunity is not tolerated for genocide, war crimes and crimes against humanity or for violations of international humanitarian law and gross violations of human rights law, and that such violations are properly investigated and appropriately sanctioned, including by bringing the perpetrators of any crimes to justice, through national mechanisms or, where appropriate, regional or international mechanisms, in accordance with international law, and for this purpose we encourage States to strengthen national judicial systems and institutions.

23. We recognize the role of the International Criminal Court in a multilateral system that aims to end impunity and establish the rule of law, and in this respect we welcome the States that have become parties to the Rome Statute of the International Criminal Court,[1] and call upon all States that are not yet parties to the Statute to consider ratifying or acceding to it, and emphasize the importance of cooperation with the Court.

24. We stress the importance of strengthened international cooperation, based on the principles of shared responsibility and in accordance with international law, in order to dismantle illicit networks and counter the world drug problem and transnational organized crime, including money-laundering, trafficking in persons, trafficking in arms and other forms of organized crime, all of which threaten national security and undermine sustainable development and the rule of law.

25. We are convinced of the negative impact of corruption, which obstructs economic growth and development, erodes public confidence, legitimacy and transparency and hinders the making of fair and effective laws, as well as their administration, enforcement and adjudication, and therefore stress the importance of the rule of law as an essential element in addressing and preventing corruption, including by strengthening cooperation among States concerning criminal matters.

26. We reiterate our strong and unequivocal condemnation of terrorism in all its forms and manifestations, committed by whomever, wherever and for whatever purposes, as it constitutes one of the most serious threats to international peace and security; we reaffirm that all measures used in the fight against terrorism must be in compliance with the obligations of States under international law, including the Charter of the United Nations, in particular the purposes and principles thereof, and relevant conventions and protocols, in particular human rights law, refugee law and humanitarian law.

---

[1] United Nations, *Treaty Series*, vol. 2187, No. 38544.

II

27. We recognize the positive contribution of the General Assembly, as the chief deliberative and representative organ of the United Nations, to the rule of law in all its aspects through policymaking and standard setting, and through the progressive development of international law and its codification.

28. We recognize the positive contribution of the Security Council to the rule of law while discharging its primary responsibility for the maintenance of international peace and security.

29. Recognizing the role under the Charter of the United Nations of effective collective measures in maintaining and restoring international peace and security, we encourage the Security Council to continue to ensure that sanctions are carefully targeted, in support of clear objectives and designed carefully so as to minimize possible adverse consequences, and that fair and clear procedures are maintained and further developed.

30. We recognize the positive contribution of the Economic and Social Council to strengthening the rule of law, pursuing the eradication of poverty and furthering the economic, social and environmental dimensions of sustainable development.

31. We recognize the positive contribution of the International Court of Justice, the principal judicial organ of the United Nations, including in adjudicating disputes among States, and the value of its work for the promotion of the rule of law; we reaffirm the obligation of all States to comply with the decisions of the International Court of Justice in cases to which they are parties; and we call upon States that have not yet done so to consider accepting the jurisdiction of the International Court of Justice in accordance with its Statute. We also recall the ability of the relevant organs of the United Nations to request advisory opinions from the International Court of Justice.

32. We recognize the contributions of the International Tribunal for the Law of the Sea, as well as other international courts and tribunals, in advancing the rule of law at the international and national levels.

33. We commend the work of the International Law Commission in advancing the rule of law at the international level through the progressive development of international law and its codification.

34. We recognize the essential role of parliaments in the rule of law at the national level, and welcome the interaction among the United Nations, national parliaments and the Inter-Parliamentary Union.

35. We are convinced that good governance at the international level is fundamental for strengthening the rule of law, and stress the importance of continuing efforts to revitalize the General Assembly, to reform the Security Council and to strengthen the Economic and Social Council, in accordance with relevant resolutions and decisions.

36. We take note of the important decisions on reform of the governance structures, quotas and voting rights of the Bretton Woods institutions, better reflecting current realities and enhancing the voice and participation of developing countries, and we reiterate the importance of the reform of the governance of those institutions in order to deliver more effective, credible, accountable and legitimate institutions.

III

37. We reaffirm that States shall abide by all their obligations under international law, and stress the need to strengthen support to States, upon their request, in the national implementation of their respective international obligations through enhanced technical assistance and capacity-building.

38. We stress the importance of international cooperation and invite donors, regional, subregional and other intergovernmental organizations, as well as relevant civil society actors, including non-governmental organizations, to provide, at the request of States, technical assistance and capacity-building, including education and training on rule of law-related issues, as well as to share practices and lessons learned on the rule of law at the international and national levels.

39. We take note of the report of the Secretary-General entitled "Delivering justice: programme of action to strengthen the rule of law at the national and international levels".[2]

40. We request the Secretary-General to ensure greater coordination and coherence among the United Nations entities and with donors and recipients to improve the effectiveness of rule of law capacity-building activities.

41. We emphasize the importance of continuing our consideration and promotion of the rule of law in all its aspects, and to that end we decide to pursue our work in the General Assembly to develop further the linkages between the rule of law and the three main pillars of the United Nations: peace and security, human rights and development. To that end, we request the Secretary-General to propose ways and means of developing, with wide stakeholder participation, further such linkages, and to include this in his report to the Assembly at its sixty-eighth session.

42. We acknowledge the efforts to strengthen the rule of law through voluntary pledges in the context of the high-level meeting, and encourage States that have not done so to consider making pledges individually or jointly, based on their national priorities, including pledges aimed at sharing knowledge, best practices and enhancing international cooperation, including regional and South-South cooperation.

3rd plenary meeting
24 September 2012

---

[2] A/66/749.

United Nations

General Assembly

A/66/74

Distr.: General
16 March 2012

Original: English

Sixty-sixth session
Agenda item 83
The rule of law at the national and international levels

Delivering justice: programme of action to strengthen the rule of law at the national and international levels

Report of the Secretary-General

Summary

Respect for the rule of law at the international and national levels is central to ensuring the predictability and legitimacy of international relations, and for delivering just outcomes in the daily life of all individuals. While responsibility for strengthening the rule of law lies with Member States and their citizens, the United Nations is ideally placed to support Member States' efforts and to provide integrated and effective assistance. To galvanize collective efforts to strengthen the rule of law at the national and international levels, the Secretary-General proposes that the General Assembly adopt a programme of action for the rule of law, agree to a process to develop clear rule of law goals and adopt other key mechanisms to enhance dialogue on the rule of law. Member States should also take the occasion of the high-level meeting of the General Assembly on the topic "The rule of law at the national and international levels" during the sixty-seventh session to make individual pledges related to the rule of law.

I. Introduction

1. The global system is coming under unprecedented stress from interconnected and complex transformations in our human and physical geography. Environmental degradation, rapid urbanization, conflict, severe income inequalities and exclusion of vulnerable groups pose major challenges to human development and security. Robust principles are needed to underpin the management of our future. The rule of law is a core principle of governance that ensures justice and fairness, values that are essential to humanity. The rule of law is central to the vision of the Secretary-General for the coming five years, and must guide our collective response to a fast-changing world.

2. The United Nations defines the rule of law as a principle of governance in which all persons, institutions and entities, public and private, including the State itself, are accountable to laws that are publicly promulgated, equally enforced and independently adjudicated, and which are consistent with international human rights norms and standards. It requires, as well, measures to ensure adherence to the principles of supremacy of law, equality before the law, accountability to the law, fairness in the application of the law, separation of powers, participation in decision-making, legal certainty, avoidance of arbitrariness and procedural and legal transparency (see S/2004/616).

3. At the international level, the rule of law accords predictability and legitimacy to the actions of States, strengthens their sovereign equality and underpins the responsibility of a State to all individuals within its territory and subject to its jurisdiction. Full implementation of the obligations set forth in the Charter of the United Nations and in other international instruments, including the international human rights framework, is central to collective efforts to maintain international peace and security, effectively address emerging threats and close off accountability gaps for international crimes.

4. At the national level, the rule of law is at the heart of the social contract between the State and individuals under its jurisdiction, and ensures that justice permeates society at every level. The rule of law guarantees the protection of the full range of human rights, brings citizens and non-citizens alike legitimate avenues of recourse in cases of abuses of power and allows for the peaceful and fair resolution of disputes. The rule of law is ensured by national institutions that can generate and implement clear, public and just laws, and that provide fair, equitable and accountable public services to all people equally. Strengthening the rule of law fosters an environment that facilitates sustainable human development and the protection and empowerment of women, children and vulnerable groups, such as internally displaced persons, stateless persons, refugees and migrants.

5. While responsibility for ensuring the rule of law at the international and national levels lies with Member States and their citizens, the United Nations can assist in strengthening it. Such assistance must be in line with the internationally agreed normative framework, but must also be led by national aspirations and anchored in the national context.

6. Each of the principal organs of the United Nations, including the Secretariat and its various departments and offices, in addition to the United Nations funds and programmes, engages in a wide range of rule of law activities. Many other multilateral actors and bilateral donors, private foundations and non-governmental

organizations are also involved in such activities. The breadth of the rule of law and the number of actors involved create challenges in prioritization, coordination and coherence.

7. To address these challenges, the Secretary-General has identified key commitments to be made by Member States and the United Nations to strengthen the rule of law at the national and international levels. These commitments are set out below in the form of a programme of action, which the Secretary-General proposes for adoption during the sixty-seventh session of the General Assembly at the high-level meeting on the topic "The rule of law at the national and international levels".

8. Looking ahead, the Secretary-General firmly believes that it is crucial for Member States to agree on key goals in relation to the rule of law, with corresponding targets, so that Member States and the United Nations have clear objectives towards which to work. The Secretary-General proposes that Member States agree to embark on this process at the high-level meeting.

9. The Secretary-General also proposes the adoption at the high-level meeting of other mechanisms aimed at strengthening dialogue on the rule of law at the international and national levels. Lastly, to make full use of the unique opportunity afforded by the high-level meeting, the Secretary-General proposes that Member States make individual pledges on the rule of law based on national priorities.

II. Programme of action

10. The Secretary-General proposes that Member States and the United Nations make a number of the commitments set out below, which are aimed at addressing the current challenges in strengthening the rule of law at the international and national levels. They take the form of a programme of action aimed at creating a common agenda for all Member States and the United Nations so that future discussions in this broad area can be more effectively structured and collective action better targeted.

A. Strengthening the rule of law at the international level

1. Increasing compliance with international law

(a) Strengthening compliance in the context of the United Nations

11. The Charter of the United Nations is the foundation of the rule of law at the international level. It is applicable to all Member States equally and to the principal organs of the United Nations. In addition, Member States are bound by the wider body of international law. In this respect, it is important for the Security Council, in addition to the other principal organs of the United Nations, to fully adhere to applicable international law and basic rule of law principles to ensure the legitimacy of their actions. In this connection:

(a) Member States and the principal organs of the United Nations must commit themselves to applying the Charter of the United Nations and the wider body of international law consistently and even-handedly in their policies and practices;

(b) The Secretary-General encourages Member States to bring forward and finalize intergovernmental discussions on Security Council reform;

(c) The Secretary-General fully accepts that relevant international law, notably international human rights, humanitarian and refugee law, is binding on the activities of the United Nations Secretariat, and is committed to complying with the corresponding obligations;

(d) The Secretary-General fully supports the new system of administration of justice and will ensure that the principles of the rule of law are consistently applied throughout the United Nations.

(b) Ensuring national implementation

12. The body of international norms and standards developed under the auspices of the United Nations remains one of the Organization's greatest achievements. While there are more areas in which law-making would be valuable, the real challenge lies in the implementation of the existing legal framework. Respect for this framework is poor, violations frequent and the political will to ensure consistent compliance too weak. The technical and financial capacities required to fulfil obligations are often limited. In this connection:

(a) Member States should ratify or accede to international treaties to which they are not yet party, and review and remove any reservations to treaties to which they are party;

(b) Member States should consistently and fully implement international legal instruments, including through specific national action plans, backed by political will and financial commitments;

(c) Where compliance with international obligations is hampered by capacity deficits, Member States should commit themselves to seeking international assistance from bilateral and multilateral assistance providers;

(d) The Secretary-General commits himself to providing an integrated response to requests by Member States for assistance in the implementation of their international obligations.

(c) Strengthening treaty bodies

13. Many international instruments include mechanisms that review Member States' compliance. Such mechanisms provide an essential tool to strengthen implementation and highlight capacity gaps. Support for treaty monitoring bodies should be strengthened and their recommendations consistently implemented. In this connection:

(a) Member States should commit themselves to allocating adequate resources to treaty body mechanisms, to regularly fulfilling their reporting requirements and to implementing their findings and recommendations;

(b) Where failure to report or to implement recommendations stems from capacity deficits, Member States should commit themselves to seeking international assistance;

(c) Bilateral and multilateral assistance providers should integrate support for the implementation of recommendations of treaty body mechanisms into their rule of law assistance budgeting and planning;

(d) The Secretary-General stands ready to provide an integrated response to requests by Member States for assistance.

2. Strengthening international dispute resolution

14. One of the central features of the rule of law at the international level is the ability of Member States to have recourse to international adjudicative mechanisms to settle their disputes peacefully, without the threat or use of force. Unfortunately, reluctance by some States to consistently use international adjudicative bodies and jurisdictional barriers to them have contributed to concerns that the international legal system is not equally accessible to all and that international law is selectively applied.

(a) Strengthening the International Court of Justice and its role in international relations

15. The International Court of Justice remains the only judicial forum before which Member States can bring virtually any legal dispute concerning international law. No other forum's jurisdiction is potentially as far-reaching as that of the Court, yet the Court is competent to hear a case only if the States concerned have accepted its jurisdiction. Such an acceptance can take the form of the conclusion of an ad hoc agreement to submit a specific dispute to the Court or of a jurisdictional clause of a treaty. The Court's jurisdiction can also derive from the optional declarations accepting such jurisdiction as compulsory. Such optional declarations are the best way of ensuring that all inter-State disputes are settled peacefully. To date, however, only 66 Member States have accepted as compulsory the jurisdiction of the Court. In this connection:

(a) Member States should accept as compulsory the jurisdiction of the International Court of Justice;

(b) The Secretary-General will launch a campaign to increase the number of Member States that accept as compulsory the jurisdiction of the International Court of Justice.

16. The General Assembly and the Security Council have the ability to refer any legal question to the Court for an advisory opinion, as do other organs of the United Nations and the specialized agencies when authorized to do so by the General Assembly. This enables the principal organs of the United Nations to ensure that any action that they take is in accordance with the Charter and international law, increasing the legitimacy of their actions. In practice, however, these advisory opinions are rarely sought. In this connection:

The General Assembly, the Security Council and other organs of the United Nations, as applicable, should commit themselves to making greater use of their ability to request advisory opinions from the International Court of Justice.

(b) **Strengthening other international adjudicative bodies**

17. International adjudicative bodies themselves are often underresourced and do not have the necessary political support, especially in view of their lack of enforcement mechanisms. Accordingly, the non-implementation of decisions of such bodies is an enduring problem. In this connection:

(a) Member States should resolve to provide international adjudicative bodies with sufficient resources for them to deal with their caseloads efficiently;

(b) Member States should commit themselves to complying systematically with all final and binding decisions of international adjudicative bodies.

B. Strengthening the rule of law at the national level

1. Improving service delivery

(a) **Effective and equitable delivery**

18. A strong rule of law relies on effective and equitable delivery of public services to all individuals within a jurisdiction, without discrimination, in line with internationally accepted norms and standards. Such public services include policing, criminal justice, corrections, civil and administrative justice, legal aid and assistance and law-making. Ensuring equitable access to these services may require the adoption of special measures for marginalized and otherwise vulnerable groups and for victims and witnesses of specific crimes, such as sexual and gender-based crimes, or those in need of international protection. The legitimacy of the State can be compromised by failure to deliver just, equitable and effective services that ensure the rule of law. In this connection:

(a) Member States should take all necessary steps to provide services that ensure the rule of law in a fair, effective, non-discriminatory and accountable manner. Such services must meet international standards and be available and accessible nationwide. Special measures must be taken to ensure that women, children and vulnerable groups enjoy full access to services related to the rule of law, and that those services respond to their rights and needs;

(b) Member States should commit themselves to supporting legal aid and assistance services, including to the poorest and most vulnerable.

(b) **Accountable and transparent delivery**

19. Within justice, security and law-making institutions, it is important to enhance transparency, accountability and oversight, and to widen participation in decision-making processes, in order to build public confidence and trust. In this connection:

Member States should ensure that their legal frameworks include basic principles of open government, such as fiscal transparency, access to information, disclosures related to public officials, accountability, remedies and oversight mechanisms, protection measures for whistle-blowers and witnesses, and public engagement in policy and decision-making, and that such legal frameworks are effectively implemented.

(c) **National budgeting and planning**

20. Proper resourcing, budgeting, planning and management are also key to ensuring greater levels of competency that lead to public confidence in justice, security and law-making institutions. In this connection:

(a) Member States should ensure that rule of law institutions receive an adequate share of the national budget, and have effective planning and management structures in place, so as to execute their functions in a professional and accountable manner, fairly and independently, free of corruption and bias;

(b) Member States should consider preparing and publishing multi-year national rule of law strategies.

(d) **National data collection**

21. Data collection and analysis are critical to strengthening service delivery, and enable the creation of baselines against which policies can be developed and action targeted towards priority areas. In this connection:

(a) Member States should devote greater resources to enhancing the capacity of national institutions to systematically collect and analyse data related to the rule of law, such as crime rates, sentencing patterns, average time for completion of trials, pretrial detention rates, percentage of population using civil courts, rates and speed of enforcement of court decisions, and the use of tools such as public perception surveys in respect of the rule of law sector, in line with internationally accepted norms and standards of data protection. Such efforts need to ensure that all data are disaggregated by sex in order to inform delivery that meets the needs of all people;

(b) Member States should facilitate the implementation of impact monitoring tools to observe changes in the performance and fundamental characteristics of justice institutions.

(e) **Civil society**

22. The rule of law is strengthened when all individuals are empowered to claim their rights, to request effective remedies and to express legitimate demands on public institutions for accountability in the fair and just delivery of public services. Civil society organizations, including professional associations of lawyers, prosecutors and judges, academic and policy research institutions, paralegal organizations and advocacy organizations focusing on the rule of law, all make important contributions to strengthening services that ensure the rule of law, especially by empowering and informing individuals. In this connection:

Member States should commit themselves to granting all individuals their full right to association and assembly, and to supporting civil society organizations and giving them the necessary legislative and political space to thrive.

(f) **Traditional and informal justice systems**

23. Member States may have justice mechanisms based on tradition, custom or religion operating alongside State institutions. These systems can play an important part in the delivery of justice services, including the adjudication and determination of disputes. In this connection:

(a) Member States and the United Nations should ensure that all laws and justice mechanisms, including traditional and informal justice mechanisms, are in line with international norms and standards;

(b) Member States should develop strategies for clarifying and strengthening the relationship between traditional and informal justice systems and formal justice systems;

(c) Member States should develop strategies for ensuring that everyone, particularly women and those belonging to vulnerable or otherwise marginalized groups, enjoys equal access to justice within all justice delivery mechanisms.

2. **Supporting peace and security in conflict and post-conflict situations**

24. In conflict and post-conflict situations, the United Nations supports rule of law initiatives that are indispensable for the establishment of peace and security. High-level political and strategic engagement by the United Nations on rule of law issues is combined with initiatives for building the capacity and integrity of key national justice and security institutions, including the police, the judicial system and prisons. Broadly, assistance is provided in ensuring accountability and reinforcing norms, building confidence in justice and security institutions and promoting gender. It also includes innovative mechanisms, such as the prosecution support cells in the Democratic Republic of the Congo, which have been established to assist national authorities in the prosecution of serious crimes. It is of paramount importance to recognize the critical contribution that justice institutions make to the establishment of peace and security in conflict and post-conflict situations, and support should be provided in a commensurate and well-sequenced manner.

25. While there is an increased focus on strengthening the rule of law in conflict and post-conflict settings, the human and financial resources required to implement activities are often lacking and critical capacity gaps persist in key areas. The steering committee on civilian capacity in the aftermath of conflict is working to address these gaps through strengthened partnerships with Member States, civil society and other multilateral partners, particularly in the global South, and with greater clarity and accountability in United Nations support. In addition, there are limited empirical data on the strength and effectiveness of key rule of law institutions. Member States should be encouraged to make sufficient resources available, especially when rule of law initiatives have been explicitly mandated by the Security Council. In this connection:

(a) Member States should nominate civilian justice experts to support United Nations initiatives in the rule of law sector in conflict and post-conflict situations;

(b) Member States should support and fund the development and implementation of multi-year joint United Nations programmes for strengthening the rule of law in conflict and post-conflict settings, and should support with human and financial resources innovative mechanisms such as the prosecution support cells;

(c) Member States should enhance resources for rule of law activities carried out in the context of United Nations peacekeeping operations and special political missions, including voluntary contributions to rule of law actions implemented by relevant United Nations entities, agencies, funds and programmes;

(d) Member States should support the use of the United Nations Rule of Law Indicators as a non-ranking, key instrument for measuring the strengths and effectiveness of law enforcement, judicial and correctional institutions in conflict and post-conflict environments.

3. **Fostering an enabling environment for sustainable human development**

26. Sustainable human development is facilitated by a strong rule of law. The provision and implementation of stable and predictable legal frameworks for businesses and labour stimulate employment by promoting entrepreneurship and the growth of small and medium-sized enterprises, and attracting public and private investment, including foreign direct investment. The link between economic development and the rule of law has long been established. Rising inequalities in wealth within and among countries are now a key concern with the potential to weaken and destabilize societies. The United Nations supports the development of a holistic sustainable human development agenda that addresses the challenges related to inclusive growth, social protection and the environment. In such an agenda, the rule of law must play a critical role in ensuring equal protection and access to opportunities.

(a) **Fostering economic growth**

27. Member States should renew their focus on the rule of law to foster enabling environments for sustainable economic growth. Such growth must be equitable, inclusive and socially responsible in order to create sufficient stability for poverty reduction and peacebuilding initiatives to take root. In this connection:

(a) Member States must resolve to develop and implement adequate legal frameworks to boost entrepreneurship and public and private sector investment, and for the development of small and medium-sized enterprises;

(b) A number of conventions and other legal texts in the domain of trade, investment and development have been developed in the context of the United Nations, and Member States should consider adopting and implementing these. Where implementation is hampered by capacity deficits, Member States must commit themselves to seeking international assistance and to providing adequate funding for such assistance;

(c) Member States must resolve to take steps to encourage employment and implement internationally agreed labour norms and standards, including for those individuals employed in the informal sectors.

(b) **Fighting corruption**

28. Corruption is a challenge that needs to be addressed by all Member States, particularly since there is a strong link between low levels of corruption and economic and social development. Under the auspices of the United Nations, Member States have created a strong normative framework to meet this challenge, and the focus must now be on universal adherence to the framework, and its full implementation. In this connection:

(a) Member States must consider ratifying the United Nations Convention against Corruption and fully implementing its provisions, making use of the peer review mechanism established by the Conference of the States Parties to the Convention;

(b) Bilateral and multilateral assistance providers should integrate into their rule of law budgeting and planning support for the technical assistance needs of Member States, as identified through the peer review mechanism of the United Nations Convention against Corruption.

(c) **Protecting housing, land and property rights**

29. The equitable and transparent administration of housing, land and property based on rule of law principles is key to economic, social and political stability. Serious deficits in this area have caused many violent conflicts and prolonged displacement. In this connection:

Member States should resolve to put in place and fully implement housing, land and property governance systems that effectively protect international social and economic rights, with particular emphasis on ensuring women's equal rights to housing, land and property, including through succession and inheritance.

(d) **Creating and maintaining civic records**

30. Ensuring appropriate civil registration and keeping comprehensive civic records is central to legal recognition by the State and equality before the law, and enables individuals to participate in economic and political processes, seek State protection and to gain access to public services such as health and education. In this connection:

Member States should resolve to establish effective systems for free and universal birth registration, and for citizenship and other civic records, which are fully accessible to all.

4. **Empowering women and children**

31. Women worldwide face violence, the denial of basic rights and discrimination, often compounded by poverty, age and legal status. Weak legal frameworks and gender and age biases of State actors abet discriminatory policies and practices of institutions, limiting women and children's access to legal redress and discouraging women and children from reporting crimes against them.

(a) **Empowering women**

32. The marginalization of women negatively affects economic growth and social welfare. Women are key actors for development in their communities and must be empowered to use the law to uphold their interests, including by fully participating in rule of law institutions. In this connection:

(a) Member States should resolve to repeal discriminatory legislation and to adopt appropriate legal frameworks to prevent discrimination against women;

(b) Member States should commit themselves to actively promoting equal access to justice, including by removing all obstacles to services that women face, and to putting in place positive measures to enhance access to these services;

(c) Member States should also resolve to increase the participation of women in the delivery of services that ensure the rule of law, including by establishing minimum quotas in relevant professions;

(d) Member States should increase the amount of funding allocated to gender-responsive rule of law assistance initiatives.

(b) Empowering children

33. The way in which children are treated by national legal, social welfare, justice and security institutions is integral to the development of the rule of law at the national level. Justice for children aims to ensure full application of international norms and standards for all children who come into contact with justice and related systems as victims, witnesses and alleged offenders, or for other reasons where judicial, State administrative or non-State adjudicatory intervention is needed (for example, regarding their care, custody or protection). Important progress notwithstanding, girls and boys are still to be viewed as full stakeholders in rule of law initiatives. Given the strong cultural dimension of the rule of law, ensuring child rights education and legal awareness for all children, and for families and communities, is key for the long-term growth of the rule of law.

34. The relevant provisions of the Convention on the Rights of the Child and other international legal instruments related to justice for children have yet to be systematically reflected in broader policy reform, programmes and other efforts to strengthen the rule of law at the national level. In this connection:

(a) Member States should resolve to regard the rights of girls and boys as integral to their initiatives to strengthen the rule of law;

(b) Member States should commit themselves to putting in place adequate policies to protect children, beginning with the establishment of systems for free and universal birth registration, and ensuring that age assessment processes fully respect the rights and best interests of the child;

(c) Member States should resolve not to use detention in respect of girls and boys, except as a last resort, and should develop appropriate diversion programmes and alternatives to detention.

C. Strengthening the nexus between the national and international levels

35. Some threats and crimes, while committed on national territory, are addressed through international legal mechanisms. It is therefore important to strengthen the nexus between the rule of law at the national and international levels.

1. Establishing the age of accountability

36. The commission of international crimes and other gross violations of human rights undermines the fabric of societies and destabilizes affected States and their regions, threatening international peace and security. In the aftermath of such crimes and violations, ensuring accountability and providing all victims with the right to an effective remedy giving redress and adequate reparations for the atrocities

committed against them are key to increasing public trust in justice and security institutions, and to building the rule of law and sustainable peace.

(a) **Ensuring investigations and prosecutions**

37. Member States are responsible for investigating, prosecuting and trying, or extraditing, perpetrators of international crimes and other gross violations of human rights. The commission of such crimes and violations anywhere in the world is of legitimate concern to every Member State, the United Nations and the international community as a whole. In this connection:

(a) All Member States must commit themselves to ensuring accountability for international crimes and other gross violations of human rights;

(b) Member States should not take measures that prevent accountability, such as granting or endorsing amnesties for international crimes and other gross violations of human rights;

(c) Member States in whose jurisdiction international crimes and other gross violations of human rights have occurred, or Member States of which the person accused of the crime is a national, must support politically and financially domestic prosecutions of alleged perpetrators of international crimes and other gross violations of human rights, while guaranteeing the full judicial, prosecutorial and investigative independence of these processes;

(d) Where a Member State with jurisdiction over international crimes and other gross violations of human rights cannot or will not investigate or prosecute crimes and violations, the State concerned should consider referring the matter to an appropriate regional or international accountability mechanism, or extraditing the alleged perpetrator to any country that has claimed jurisdiction over the violations;

(e) Where a Member State with jurisdiction over international crimes and other gross violations of human rights cannot or will not exercise jurisdiction, other Member States should explore avenues for exercising their own jurisdiction and make corresponding extradition requests.

38. Children who are accused of international crimes and gross violations of human rights require special consideration. In this connection:

(a) Where international crimes and gross violations of human rights are allegedly committed by children associated with armed forces or armed groups, Member States should regard the children primarily as victims and not as perpetrators;

(b) Member States should not prosecute, punish or threaten with prosecution or punishment children who have been associated with armed forces or armed groups solely for their membership of those forces or groups;

(c) When children engage as witnesses in judicial or non-judicial accountability processes, Member States should commit themselves to putting in place protection procedures and legal safeguards to protect their rights before, during and after their testimony or statement.

(b) Strengthening national capacities

39. Inadequate capacity within domestic institutions fosters impunity for the perpetrators of international crimes and other gross violations of human rights. The United Nations has developed innovative mechanisms to assist national authorities in investigating, prosecuting and trying alleged perpetrators of such crimes and violations, for instance through capacity-building of police to investigate sexual and gender-based violence cases, and the prosecution support cells used in the Democratic Republic of the Congo, as mandated by the Security Council in its resolutions 1925 (2010) and 1991 (2011). In this connection:

(a) Member States must resolve to strengthen their national systems to conduct investigations and prosecutions of alleged perpetrators of international crimes and other gross violations of human rights, and to seek international assistance to do so, where necessary. Specific efforts should be made to build the necessary capacity to investigate, prosecute and try sexual and gender-based crimes, and crimes against children;

(b) Bilateral and multilateral assistance providers should integrate into their rule of law assistance support for strengthening national capacity to pursue domestic proceedings for international crimes and gross violations of human rights, and ensure that such assistance is nationally and locally driven;

(c) The Secretary-General will ensure that the United Nations is able to provide an integrated response to any request by Member States for assistance.

(c) Other accountability mechanisms

40. In addition to the primary role of national authorities to punish those responsible for international crimes and other gross violations of human rights, international and hybrid criminal tribunals have played an important role in closing the accountability gap. Commissions of inquiry and fact-finding missions have also been increasingly viewed as effective tools to draw out facts necessary for wider accountability and transitional justice efforts. Similarly, in the case of children in situations of armed conflict, the monitoring and reporting mechanism on children and armed conflict, as mandated by the Security Council in its resolutions 1612 (2005), 1882 (2009) and 1998 (2011), is an important tool to galvanize accountability efforts for grave crimes against children. With regard to women, peace and security, new mechanisms have been established by the Security Council in resolutions 1888 (2009) and 1960 (2010). In this connection:

(a) Member States should encourage and support national and international commissions of inquiry and fact-finding missions, established in accordance with international standards, and support the implementation of their recommendations. Member States with seats on the Security Council and the Human Rights Council have particular responsibility in this regard;

(b) Member States should cooperate fully with international and hybrid accountability mechanisms established by the United Nations or with its support;

(c) Member States that are party to the Rome Statute of the International Criminal Court must incorporate the Rome Statute into national legislation and should discharge their obligations to cooperate fully with the Court;

(d) All Member States not party to the Rome Statute should consider ratifying it;

(e) Where a Member State with jurisdiction over international crimes cannot or will not exercise jurisdiction, and is not a party to the Rome Statute, Member States that are members of the Security Council should consider referring the situation to the Prosecutor of the International Criminal Court, under Chapter VII of the Charter of the United Nations.

(d) Focusing on victims

41. Victims must take a central place in any system of accountability for international crimes and other gross violations of human rights. In this connection:

(a) Member States should resolve to support, financially and politically, transitional justice mechanisms aimed at establishing the truth, reconciliation and furthering accountability in relation to the commission of international crimes and other gross violations of human rights, and to follow up on the recommendations and decisions of such mechanisms;

(b) Member States should consider ways to effectively meet their obligations to grant remedies and reparations to victims of international crimes and other gross violations of human rights, with special consideration for groups most affected by these crimes and those who have traditionally been excluded from or marginalized in reparations programmes, such as victims of sexual and gender-based violence;

(c) Member States should consider developing comprehensive victim and witness protection programmes covering international crimes and gross violations of human rights.

2. Addressing transnational threats

42. Transnational threats, such as organized crime, piracy and trafficking, are both the cause and consequence of a weak rule of law environment, and pose a serious challenge to the legitimacy of the State and to international peace and security. Networks of organized criminal groups are challenging the authority of the State. Law enforcement authorities can lag behind organized criminal groups in organizational skills and employment of new technology. Insufficient cooperation among law enforcement authorities within and across borders hinders progress. At the same time, growing levels of corruption facilitate transnational organized crime by weakening economies and draining Government revenues, thereby reducing people's confidence in rule of law institutions.

(a) Implementing the normative framework

43. A solid normative framework has been put in place to fight transnational threats, through the United Nations Convention against Transnational Organized Crime and the three optional protocols that supplement it: the Protocol to Prevent, Suppress and Punish Trafficking in Persons, Especially Women and Children; the Protocol against the Smuggling of Migrants by Land, Sea and Air; and the Protocol against the Illicit Manufacturing of and Trafficking in Firearms, Their Parts and Components and Ammunition.

44. In addition to international and regional anti-terrorism conventions, all Member States have agreed on a coordinated and comprehensive response to terrorism at the national, regional and global levels through the adoption, and subsequent reaffirmation, of the United Nations Global Counter-Terrorism Strategy by the General Assembly (see resolution 60/288). Through the Global Strategy, which includes a plan of action, all Member States have made respect for all human rights and the rule of law the fundamental basis of efforts to combat terrorism.

45. Focus must now be on universal adherence to this normative framework and its full implementation. In this connection:

(a) All Member States should consider ratifying or acceding to the United Nations Convention against Transnational Organized Crime and its optional protocols, in particular the Protocol to Prevent, Suppress and Punish Trafficking in Persons, Especially Women and Children;

(b) Member States that are party to the United Nations Convention against Transnational Organized Crime and its protocols must fully implement this normative framework in their jurisdictions, and cooperate with other Member States as required;

(c) Member States should commit themselves to adopting comprehensive strategies to combat trafficking, including protection and prevention measures, efforts to prosecute perpetrators and increased access to a full range of reparations measures, including legal redress for victims of trafficking;

(d) Member States should strengthen their capacity to effectively track, seize and confiscate illicit assets and proceeds of crime in order to disrupt the financial flows of organized criminal groups, and consider establishing a designated authority in charge of the management and disposal of illicit assets;

(e) Member States should implement the United Nations Global Counter-Terrorism Strategy and, in particular, develop and maintain an effective and rule of law-based national criminal justice system in order to ensure that individuals suspected of involvement in terrorist acts are brought to justice, on the basis of the principle to extradite or prosecute, in accordance with international human rights, humanitarian and refugee law, including due process guarantees.

(b) Increasing cooperation

46. There is growing acknowledgement that regional approaches are required to address transnational threats, involving close cooperation and capacity-building at both the national and regional levels. The exchange and sharing of information by national authorities are important in understanding transnational threats more fully. The problem of piracy clearly demonstrates the increasing interdependence of Member States and people in a globalized world. The human, commercial and security interests under threat engage many Member States and international and regional organizations with a stake in finding a solution. In this connection:

(a) Member States should cooperate in identifying and sharing information about specific transnational threats;

(b) Member States should establish national and regional policies and programmes to protect adolescents and young people from being used or recruited by organized crime and terrorist groups;

(c) The United Nations and Member States should commit themselves to supporting the United Nations system task force on transnational organized crime and drug trafficking as threats to security and stability, with a view to ensuring joint programming that mainstreams issues of transnational threats into conflict prevention, peacebuilding and development planning.

D. Strengthening support to Member States

47. Strengthening the rule of law is a long-term endeavour requiring the United Nations and other multilateral and bilateral actors to adopt flexible and coordinated mechanisms to assist States effectively. While progress has been made, assistance remains fragmented and its effectiveness uncertain.

1. Political engagement

48. The rule of law is at the heart of State sovereignty and national systems of governance. Consequently, efforts to strengthen the rule of law are inherently political and require the support and involvement of key national stakeholders to ensure the authority, credibility and legitimacy required for rule of law initiatives to achieve results. Assistance providers must engage in a frank political dialogue with a wide range of national stakeholders, including the appropriate Government officials, for any rule of law assistance programmes to succeed. In this connection:

(a) The Secretary-General will promote the use of rule of law compacts, or similar instruments, with national authorities so that clear objectives on rule of law assistance are agreed upon and mutual accountability defined;

(b) Within the United Nations, the Secretary-General resolves to work with senior managers, including United Nations resident coordinators and special representatives of the Secretary-General, to make the rule of law a priority in high-level dialogue with national authorities;

(c) Member States should contribute to a high-level dialogue with national stakeholders in support of agreed rule of law priorities.

2. Coordination

49. Successful support for the rule of law requires more active coordination between the United Nations, Member States and national stakeholders. Member States contribute the vast majority of donor funding for rule of law initiatives through bilateral programmes, often in parallel with multilateral efforts and national strategies. Improved coordination among bilateral programmes and multilateral donors, with national leadership and in line with nationally owned strategies, can lead to more effective and efficient use of resources. In this connection:

(a) Within the United Nations, the Secretary-General resolves to increase coordination among United Nations entities working in the rule of law sector by strengthening coordination mechanisms with enhanced mandates and reaffirming the important role of special representatives of the Secretary-General and/or resident coordinators in ensuring consistent and coherent programme delivery throughout the United Nations;

(b) Member States and the United Nations resolve to apply a joint and comprehensive approach, clearly articulating priorities and plans for sequencing interventions;

(c) Member States and the United Nations resolve to support nationally led donor coordination and consultation mechanisms that direct assistance and funding, on the basis of national rule of law strategies and priorities;

(d) Member States and the United Nations should commit themselves to enhancing assistance to build national capacity in lead ministries and other appropriate institutions to plan and coordinate the international assistance that they receive;

(e) Member States should make more consistent use of multilateral mechanisms to provide rule of law assistance.

3. **Funding**

50. Member States can provide financial incentives for coordinated joint programming between United Nations entities by channelling their funding through basket funds or other pooled funding arrangements. Joint programmes funded through multi-year pooled arrangements will support national priorities more effectively and reduce administrative and other costs to national administrations. In this connection:

(a) Within the United Nations, the Secretary-General resolves to develop and implement multi-year joint programmes for strengthening the rule of law, including police, judicial and corrections institutions, and to ensure that they are planned, funded, implemented, monitored and evaluated jointly. In countries with United Nations peacekeeping operations or special political missions, this will be based on integrated planning processes;

(b) Member States should enhance resources for United Nations rule of law assistance and commit themselves to increasing support through multi-year joint United Nations programmes with a view to ensuring comprehensive approaches.

4. **Joint assessments**

51. For Member States and the United Nations to understand the capacity gaps, and to design and agree on comprehensive rule of law assistance programmes, thorough assessments of the sector must be conducted. Joint assessments, agreed upon by the recipient State, the United Nations and all interested donors, can improve effective programming, including the development of United Nations joint programmes and workplans. Efforts should be made to mainstream this approach in rule of law assistance. In this connection:

(a) The Secretary-General is committed, in order to conduct thorough assessments of the rule of law sector, to fostering the use of existing tools and to developing new tools that are rooted in the political economy of a country and fully reflect individual complexities and power structures;

(b) Member States should consider the use of joint assessments when coordinating or delivering rule of law assistance.

5. **Monitoring and evaluation**

52. It should become a regular practice to establish baselines that can be measured to monitor and evaluate progress and assess the effectiveness of rule of law assistance. National ownership is critical in identifying indicators and supporting capacity-building for justice and security institutions to gather and assess data and measure developments. In this connection:

> As a means of strengthening the United Nations approach to measuring the effectiveness of rule of law assistance, the Secretary-General will mainstream the use of existing instruments for measuring the strengths and effectiveness of law enforcement, judicial and correctional institutions in conflict and post-conflict environments, and the use of baseline statistical surveys, benchmarking exercises and regular reporting of progress against indicators.

III. Mechanisms to strengthen the rule of law at the international and national levels

53. To strengthen the rule of law at the international and national levels, the Secretary-General proposes that the General Assembly adopt the mechanisms described below.

A. Rule of law goals

54. Developing clear, simple and common goals for the rule of law, with corresponding benchmarks and indicators measuring progress towards those goals, would be essential for Member States and the United Nations in generating collective, measurable progress towards implementing the programme of action.

55. The Millennium Development Goals have shown that, where Member States have agreed upon specific goals, the international community has been able to better prioritize actions and generate more targeted resources. Internationally agreed goals and corresponding benchmarks have proved useful in measuring progress and in constructing an inclusive national dialogue on strategies to meet those goals. The Secretary-General therefore believes that the development of common goals in the area of the rule of law is important for Member States and the United Nations. The consultative forum proposed below could be the appropriate venue to inform this process.

56. Member States may also wish to consider how progress in the attainment of rule of law goals, once agreed upon, can be effectively monitored, and how they can seek assistance in meeting the goals, where progress is lacking. A number of peer review processes are already in place in other forums, and the Secretary-General stands ready to provide lessons learned and assist Member States in any such discussions.

57. The rule of law goals should be harmonized, where possible, with existing processes. One such process, led by the International Dialogue on Peacebuilding and Statebuilding, is to develop indicators for the five peacebuilding and statebuilding goals that were endorsed by 40 Member States at the end of 2011. While the rule of law goals proposed would be broader in scope, and applicable beyond the

peacebuilding context, the Secretary-General proposes that Member States work closely with the International Dialogue so that the two processes are harmonized. The work performed by the International Dialogue could form a useful basis for developing broader rule of law goals.

58. The other pertinent process is that of the Millennium Development Goals and its follow-up after 2015. The Secretary-General notes that rule of law goals would have a positive impact on the achievement of the Millennium Development Goals by promoting a strong enabling environment. However, the two processes should initially develop separately, with a view to alignment in the future.

59. In the light of the above, the Secretary-General proposes that the General Assembly initiate a process to develop and agree on key goals for the rule of law at the international and national levels, and stands ready to support any process that Member States may agree upon in this respect.

B. Consultative forum on the rule of law

60. The many distinct stakeholders active in strengthening the rule of law currently do not meet in a structured way to discuss common policies on the rule of law, and key policymakers in the United Nations do not benefit from the full range of voices available to inform their discussions. A consultative forum could integrate the many distinct voices of relevant stakeholders into coordinated and coherent global policy advice for the United Nations and Member States on strengthening the rule of law at the international and national levels. Such a forum could also be used to generate effective South-South and triangular cooperation in the sector.

61. A consultative forum, open to all Member States, would include representatives of the relevant national authorities, such as prosecutors or judges, the United Nations, other intergovernmental organizations, regional and non-governmental organizations, academic institutions, think tanks and the private sector. The exact composition of each meeting of the forum would vary depending on the issue to be discussed, and would serve to engender transformative multi-stakeholder partnerships.

62. The forum could be guided by a steering committee, with representatives of Member States and stakeholders, and serviced by the United Nations Secretariat. The steering committee would agree on the programme of work for the forum and on the most suitable participants for each meeting of the forum. A transparent mechanism for communication between the steering committee and the stakeholders would be important to ensure participation and broad ownership of the process. The forum would submit regular reports on its work to the General Assembly.

63. The forum could also build on existing processes and link with other global initiatives such as the Global Forum on Law, Justice and Development, a multiconstituency knowledge partnership launched by the World Bank, of which the United Nations Secretariat is a founding partner.

64. In the light of the above, the Secretary-General proposes that the General Assembly mandate him to convene a multi-stakeholder consultative forum on the rule of law, which would meet periodically to discuss specific thematic issues and report to the General Assembly thereon.

C. Comprehensive intergovernmental dialogue

65. The rule of law is a principle cutting across many issues considered by the General Assembly and, consequently, efforts to strengthen the rule of law are discussed in varying dimensions in all the main committees of the General Assembly in the context of their mandates, and by other principal organs of the United Nations. This has previously led to the General Assembly taking a disjointed approach to issues related to the rule of law. The occasion of the high-level meeting affords Member States the opportunity to review how discussions on the rule of law are conducted by the General Assembly.

66. Discussion by the General Assembly in plenary meeting, which would periodically draw together the separate discussions in the main committees, would produce a more coherent and multilayered debate around the rule of law. Such discussions could be further informed by the consultative forum proposed above, as and when requested by the General Assembly. In addition, the programme of action could be periodically reviewed in the context of the plenary meetings of the General Assembly.

67. In the light of the above, the Secretary-General proposes that Member States hold periodic discussions on the rule of law in a plenary meeting of the General Assembly.

IV. Pledges

68. A number of international conferences have been used by Member States to make specific pledges that further the aims of the conference. At the international conferences of the Red Cross and Red Crescent, participants are called upon to sign voluntarily either individual or joint, specific, humanitarian commitments in the form of pledges. The Review Conference of the Rome Statute held in Kampala in 2010 was used by Member States to make specific pledges on cooperation with the International Criminal Court, or on domesticating the Rome Statute. In the Human Rights Council, Member States make specific pledges on strengthening their human rights regimes in the context of their elections to the Council.

69. Member States should take the occasion of the high-level meeting of the General Assembly to make pledges on the rule of law based on national priorities. The pledges must be short, specific and measurable and related to the programme of action outlined above.

70. In the light of the above, the Secretary-General proposes that Member States take the occasion of the high-level meeting to make individual pledges related to the programme of action.

Secretary-General Ban Ki-moon
General Assembly
24 September 2012

Remarks to High-Level Meeting of the General Assembly on the Rule of Law

L'état de droit est comme la loi de la pesanteur. C'est lui qui fait que notre monde et nos sociétés restent soudés, que l'ordre prévaut sur le chaos. Il nous rassemble autour de valeurs communes; il nous ancre dans le bien commun.

Mais contrairement à la loi de la pesanteur, l'état de droit ne se manifeste pas spontanément. Il doit être nourri par les efforts continus et concertés de dirigeants véritables.

Aujourd'hui, des chefs de gouvernement, des ministres de la justice, des procureurs généraux et des représentants de la société civile se réunissent dans cette salle pour la première fois afin de débattre exclusivement du renforcement de la justice pour les habitants de tous les pays du monde.

L'attente fut longue. Mais cela fait des dizaines d'années que l'Organisation des Nations Unies s'attelle à renforcer l'état de droit, et la réunion d'aujourd'hui reflète un mouvement mondial de plus en plus vaste réunissant de simples citoyens qui réclament la justice, le respect du principe de responsabilité et la fin de l'impunité.

Nous savons que renforcer l'état de droit, c'est consolider les trois piliers de l'Organisation des Nations Unies : la paix, le développement et les droits de l'homme.

La justice n'est pas une notion abstraite. C'est une carte d'électeur, un contrat en bonne et due forme, le badge d'un policier qui inspire la confiance et le certificat de naissance qui fait qu'une petite fille aura une existence officielle.

La veuve qui n'hérite de rien, le militant des droits de l'homme qui subit des représailles et la victime d'atteintes sexuelles, tous ont besoin de l'état de droit pour obtenir justice.

The Charter of the United Nations – the Constitution of the international community – provides indispensable tools to deepen the rule of law: the universal standard-setting power of the General Assembly … the enforcement power of the Security Council … the judicial power of the International Court of Justice.

The wider body of international law developed at the United Nations gives the international community a basis to cooperate and peacefully resolve conflicts – and the means to ensure that there is no relapse of fighting.

And with the development of accountability mechanisms, no war criminal should ever find safe harbour in the modern world.

The rule of law is also fundamental to development and achieving the Millennium Development Goals. Today's discussion should strengthen our resolve to ensure that the post-2015 international development agenda takes full account of the rule of law.

I am proud that the United Nations is promoting the rule of law in more than 150 countries.

I am grateful for the many voluntary pledges being made today.

I thank the governments that have made the commitments.

But I ask for concrete action in five specific areas.

First, I call on all States to commit to the equal application of the law at both the national and international levels. There should be no selectivity in applying resolutions, decisions and laws. We cannot allow political self-interest to undermine justice.

Second, I call on Heads of State and Government to uphold the highest standards of the rule of law in their decision making at all times. The rule of law must be the foundation for every government action.

Third, I call on all Heads of State and Government to accept the jurisdiction of the International Court of Justice.

Fourth, I urge Member States to support peace by strengthening UN initiatives in the field of the rule of law: training police, improving corrections and enhancing the judiciary in fragile and conflict-torn countries around the world.

Fifth, and fundamentally, I urge you to adopt the solemn declaration that is before you to make the most of this truly historic occasion to commit to respect for international law and justice and to an international order based on the rule of law.

Civil society plays a crucial role in holding leaders to account, and I urge you to keep pushing for action in all of these action areas to give the rule of law the place it deserves.

It is not enough to disperse our rule of law activities across the United Nations agenda. They deserve a central place in the structure of our work.

I count on you to help forge a new, structured approach to strengthening the rule of law and delivering justice so we can achieve peace, development and human rights.

Strengthening the rule of law is for every country and is in everyone's interest.

It is as essential within countries as it is among the family of nations.

Today's meeting is a milestone – but it is not an end in itself. Our challenge now is to follow up, generate momentum and continue to give a high profile to this essential foundation for a better future.

Thank you.

GENERAL ASSEMBLY
Sixty-seventh session

**High-level meeting on the rule of law
at the national and international levels
24 September 2012**

**Statement of the
International Institute of Higher Studies in Criminal Sciences (ISISC)
Non-Governmental Organization authorized by letter of the
President of the General Assembly, dated 7 September 2012**

Mr. President, Participants at the High-level meeting, Distinguished Delegates:

I start by recalling General Assembly Resolution 66/102 of 13 January 2012, which states: "...*Convinced* that the promotion of and respect for the rule of law at the national and international levels, as well as justice and good governance, should guide the activities of the United Nations and of its Member States, ..."

I also recall General Assembly Resolution A/66/749 of 16 March 2012, whose summary states:

> Respect for the rule of law at the international and national levels is central to ensuring the predictability and legitimacy of international relations, and for delivering just outcomes in the daily life of all individuals. While responsibility for strengthening the rule of law lies with Member States and their citizens, the United Nations is ideally placed to support Member States' efforts and to provide integrated and effective assistance. To galvanize efforts to strengthen the rule of law at the national and international levels, the Secretary-General proposes that the General Assembly adopt a programme of action for the rule of law, agree to a process to develop clear rule of law goals and adopt other key mechanisms to enhance dialogue on the rule of law. Member States should also take the occasion of the high-level meeting of the General Assembly on the topic "The rule of law at the national and international levels" during the sixty-seventh session to make individual pledges related to the rule of law.

I further recall the *Guidance Note of the Secretary-General: UN Approach to Rule of Law Assistance* of April 2008, which identified the important characteristics of effective rule of law assistance programs to be provided by the United Nations and others.

Mr. Chairman,

1. International civil society strongly supports the efforts of the Secretary General, the various Agencies and Bodies of the United Nations system, as well as the many governmental, inter-governmental organizations, and non-governmental organizations who support the rule of law, both in its broadest sense which encompasses the higher values of law and justice, and in its implementation at the legal and administrative levels.

2. The rule of law, in its broadest sense, encompasses many of the functions of international, inter-governmental, governmental, and non-governmental organizations. Rule of law is also about providing support for an effective legal, administrative, and social infrastructure whose ultimate purpose is to ensure the protection of the higher values of life, liberty, human dignity, equality, and justice. This approach to rule of law is indispensable in sustaining democracy and freedom.

3. Historically, rule of law has been interpreted as addressing laws and legal institutions, specifically law enforcement, prosecution, the judiciary, correctional services, and administrative legal processes. But it also encompasses preventing wrongs and providing remedies for victims, as reflected in the *Basic Principles and Guidelines on the Right to a Remedy and Reparation for Victims of Gross Violations of International Human Rights Law and Serious Violations of International Humanitarian Law* (G.A. Res. 147, U.N. Doc. A/RES/60/147 (March 21, 2006)).

4. The time has now come to focus on rule of law capacity-building at the United Nations. It is time to increase rule of law's effectiveness rather than expand its scope to include every value and goal of international and national societies. In order for this initiative to be successful, the United Nations must avoid the generalities and vagueness that seems to pervade the present trend in rule of law programing. Instead, UN Agencies and Bodies need to embrace specificity in their rule of law programs.

5. Notwithstanding the interests of the UN Agencies and Bodies engaged in rule of law programs, it is important not to compromise or diffuse the broad operational design of this new initiative by assigning different aspects to separate Agencies and Bodies in order to accommodate particular interests. The diffusion of rule of law activities between different UN Agencies and Bodies will present a challenge to the effective implementation and executive of such programs. There is already some diffusion of the administration of rule of law programs at the United Nations, which has limited their effectiveness. Further diffusing this important rule of law initiative by assigning important functions to various UN Agencies and Bodies will only increase these difficulties and limit its impact.

The following is therefore recommended:

1. The establishment of a special Council or Committee within the Secretary-General's office to coordinate the programs of all UN Agencies and Bodies involved in the funding and administration of rule of law activities.

2. The Council or Committee should represent all UN Agencies and Bodies working on rule of law issues, with a special focus on developing and applying best policies and practices across the United Nations, as well as promoting cooperation and synergy where appropriate. In addition, this Council or Committee should establish a database of national and international experts, as well as experienced professional and administrative personnel to be used by UN Agencies and Bodies working on rule of law initiatives.

3. The Council or Committee should also include representatives of inter-governmental, governmental, and non-governmental organizations in order to make use of their experiences and resources, as well as enhance cooperation and synergy where appropriate, both between themselves and with UN Agencies and Bodies.

4. The Council or Committee should encourage and support national rule of law programs, as well as enhance the efforts of donor states, inter-governmental, governmental, and non-governmental organizations, especially by sharing best practices and promoting cooperation and synergy.

5. With regard to fact-finding missions and special procedures, the Office of the High Commissioner for Human Rights, in cooperation with the Human Rights Council, should undertake the necessary steps to identify best policies and practices, and ensure greater uniformity in the operation of these fact-finding missions and special procedures. This includes, but is not limited to, developing a common, standardized database system which would make the work of fact-finding missions and special procedures more uniform and streamlined. These steps would also develop greater synergy between such bodies whenever they have similar goals or address related subjects, thereby making them more effective.

6. The Office of the High Commissioner for Human Rights should also develop guidelines for best policies and practices for national fact-finding commissions, such as the South African Truth and Reconciliation Commission, the Peruvian Truth and Reconciliation Commission, and the Bahrain Independent Commission of Inquiry. This would enhance the operations of national initiatives, and also relieve the United Nations system of the responsibility of undertaking an increasing number of such tasks.